MW00911611

Coaching the Camp Coach

Leadership Development for Small Organizations

Michael Shelton, MS, CAC, CFT

American Camping Association®

*For Donald. Living proof of the power of the brain,
the body, and the spirit to heal.*

Copyright 2003 by American Camping Association, Inc.

Printed in the United States of America

All rights reserved. No part of this book may be reproduced or transmitted in any
form or by any means, electronic or mechanical, including photocopying,
recording, or an information storage and retrieval system, without permission in
writing from the Publisher.

Cover, text design, and graphics by Hura Design, Inc.

Illustrations by Aleshia Detweiler

Copy edited by BooksCraft, Inc.

American Camping Association, Inc.
5000 State Road 67 North
Martinsville, Indiana 46151-7902
765-342-8456 National Office
800-428-CAMP Bookstore
www.ACAcamps.org

ISBN 0-87603-182-3

A CIP catalog record for this book can be obtained from the Library of Congress.

TABLE OF CONTENTS

INTRODUCTION

COACHING DEFINED

Coaching for improvement in leadership skills is assuming a role of increasing importance in the complicated lives of leaders. Chief executive officers and other high-ranking managers most often seek out leadership training. However, lower ranking members of industry are increasingly utilizing the same training. Those coached in business may now be "anyone from a $60,000 middle manager up to the CEO" (Smith, p. 126).

Unfortunately, for those working in nonprofit agencies and small businesses such as camps and outdoor education facilities, coaching is simply not feasible. The cost of such consultation, though beneficial in the long run, is far too expensive in the short term. Few nonprofit agencies or small businesses can afford coaching. The smaller the business, the less likely coaching will be offered.

This inability to obtain the services of a coach can hinder the personal and professional development of a leader. Most coaches have a background in psychology, which has innumerable applications to the world of business. Increased interpersonal and intrapersonal skills can make the difference between a good leader and a great one.

Why is there such an increase in the use of coaching? Is this a passing fad, or is there really a need for coaching? Kiel et al. lists several reasons for the necessity of coaching.

- **Leaders need, but have few opportunities for continuing, development.** It is a common belief that those who reach the ranks of management and leadership already have the necessary skills for such leadership. Katz and Miller, however, remind us that "until fairly recently, the standard industry model reflected straight-line thinking regarding leadership—put the best accountant in charge of all the financial people, the best chemist in charge of all the chemists, and so forth" (p. 110). Unfortunately, the skills and leadership style that worked so well in lower level positions may not be appropriate in the new position. Organizations have started to realize that the individual promoted because he or she demonstrates the best skills in a lower position does not automatically find success in management. Organizations now accept that they "need to develop and promote people who can lead—who can get things done through others—as opposed to taking the best person at a specific technical task away from that task and asking that person to watch others do the task" (pp. 110–111). Leadership requires specific skills that may not have been necessary or learned in the lower position.

- **Personal development seldom gets priority.** Due to multiple constraints on a leader's time and an often overwhelming workload, there is little time for personal development, even for those who recognize the need for it.

- **Self-understanding demands quality feedback.** Leaders and managers do not commonly receive critical feedback regarding their performance. Staff members who may have helpful feedback are cautious, and most often silent, in presenting the feedback. Most employees are intimidated by the idea of presenting critical information to their superiors. The higher the rank an individual has, the less quality feedback he or she will receive. Leaders must proactively seek feedback and information to augment their performance.

- **Positive individual change has a positive organizational impact.** Because leaders set the tone for an organization and have a profound effect on its success, personal development will likewise positively affect the entire system.

Coaching, as it is currently defined, consists of two components: the improvement of skills related to leadership success and the establishment of a relationship with another person that enhances the leader's psychological development. Coaching is a relationship between a person with leadership responsibility and a consultant who specializes in performance enhancement.

Goals

There are two goals for this book. The first is to offer leaders the chance to benefit from state-of-the-art psychological research. The book focuses specifically on building the intrapersonal skills that are necessary for successful self-regulation and for successful interactions with other people, particularly those that leaders supervise. The second goal is to teach leaders how to share this information with the individuals they supervise. Summer camps and fast food franchises, for example, hire numerous young people—usually individuals with minimal supervisory skills—and place them into middle-management-type positions, such as team and group leaders. I hope that those reading this book will work with these young people to increase their intrapersonal and interpersonal skills. This could occur, for example, through ongoing training sessions.

If the reader of this book is fortunate enough to be able to hire the services of an executive coach, then put this book down! You don't need it. This book is written specifically for those who want to improve their performance but cannot afford to hire a professional coach. It will in no way take the place of professional consultation. Recall that the definition of executive coaching states the need for a relationship between a leader and an outside consultant. The best this book can do is to clarify some of the common intrapersonal problems encountered by leaders and to teach the techniques used to overcome them.

This book will assist you in developing your leadership abilities through the presentation of the most recent literature on leadership, through self-evaluation in the workbook on the enclosed CD, and through an evaluation tool that will offer staff members a chance to safely present valuable feedback to you in your position as a leader. A director who completes the text, the workbook, and the evaluation will most certainly identify some of his or her strengths or weaknesses and be able to formulate a plan for ongoing self-improvement. The work required may not always be pleasant and may, on occasion, be disturbing as you come face to face with your leadership deficits.

To better enable you to integrate the accompanying workbook material with your reading of the text, a visual cue is presented when a workbook section is particularly relevant to a portion of the text (see page 38, for example).

As stated earlier, this book also has a second purpose: to assist the director in building stronger and more successful leadership skills in his staff. This cultivation of your staff is just as important as your own growth. Strong leaders need to be nurtured. Just as you are making plans for your own leadership development, a personal development plan for each supervisory staff member is also beneficial. For example, maybe Sarah needs to seek the advice of at least three people before she makes decisions. Possibly John needs to learn to deal with angry staff members more productively. Maybe Robert needs to formulate a plan on how to achieve an extra hour of sleep each night since he falls asleep during the afternoon every day. These supervisory staff members will be able to grow into better leaders through the presentation of formal didactic training materials, a self-evaluation process, and feedback from the director.

To assist with this, several trainings are included in the text. Each training can be completed in approximately an hour to ninety minutes, although all can be modified to meet a longer or shorter time frame. Unlike formal trainings that all staff members might be required to attend, such as fire safety, CPR, or missing camper protocol, these trainings are meant only for supervisory staff. They require minimal preparation. In fact, the director who has read this book and completed the accompanying workbook could already create numerous trainings to meet his or her purposes. The trainings in this book have been developed to occur in an informal setting, to require much interaction between participants, and to be presented to a small number of participants. These have not been developed for the entire camp community. They are strictly for supervisory staff and those staff whom you predict will soon be supervisors.

Chapter overviews briefly introduce the material to be covered. Anyone who has attended a workshop or a conference session lately has seen the presenter give an overview of the material prior to beginning the actual work. This is not simply a time killer. A brief synopsis in advance enables the brain to better organize the material for increased comprehension and future recall. Similarly, there is a brief review of key points at the end of each chapter.

The Models for the Book

Coaching can be used to improve many areas of leadership. The focus of this book will be on coaching for performance. This refers to increasing general functioning and effectiveness in a present leadership position. Its purpose is to familiarize readers with the most recent findings of the different subfields of psychology and their applications to management and leadership. By learning how your internal thoughts and feelings affect overt behavior, you can better regulate yourself and increase effective leadership. Most leaders are unaware of how their own personal psychological makeup affects their success, either for the good or the bad.

There are two models underlying this book, and both make use of a pyramid structure to graphically illustrate their points. The first is by Bompa and is a highly regarded approach to training world-class athletes (Figure I.1).

Athletes must ascend through several levels of necessary and essential training approaches to achieve maximum performance. The first level, multilateral development, consists of overall physical development, including speed, flexibility, coordination, and endurance. Without such a base, the athlete will not likely succeed in the next level of training. The next level of

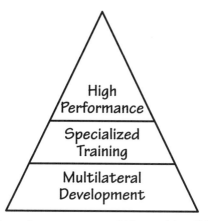

Figure I.1 This performance pyramid is used in athletic training.
Adapted, by permission, from T. O. Bompa, 1999, *Periodization*, 4th ed. (Champaign, IL: Human Kinetics), p. 31.

the pyramid, specialized training, focuses on development for the specific sport that the person will be mastering. Each sport requires specific training. An individual training for football would train differently than one whose sport is skiing. The highest level of this pyramid is high performance. At this level, the individual is already an accomplished and proficient athlete and focuses on ongoing improvement and expertise in the chosen sport. In summary, an athlete begins his or her career through general physical development and advances to increasing specialization and capability in the chosen sport.

Should the emerging athlete fail to recognize this progression, he or she will soon be injured and unable to function well. The athlete may also become discouraged by not understanding the inadequate foundation of training.

Like athletes, leaders must also have a period of general development in which they acquire the necessary physical, mental, and emotional skills that will be necessary as they ascend in leadership. As leaders move into the specialized development level, they begin to learn leader-specific material such as organizational dynamics and culture, employment law, team building, entrepreneurship, etc. A leader will then advance into the highest level of leadership in which he or she focuses on continued improvement within the confines of a particular field. A leader would continue to improve performance in a camp setting differently than the leader of a multibillion dollar industry. In essence, all leaders require a basic knowledge and proficiency of intrapersonal and interpersonal skills before they begin to grow into capable individuals who direct specific industries or organizations.

Leaders who fail to recognize this progression may find themselves in situations where their skills do not meet the needs of the situation. Subsequently, their leadership will be ineffective. Professional failure may follow unless appropriate coaching occurs. Again, the purpose of this book is to provide such coaching for those who would be unable to get training elsewhere.

The next model underlying this book is that of Loehr and Schwartz . Their model presents an approach to developing the basic skills that comprise the general multilateral development of the first model. In their article, "The Making of a Corporate Athlete," the authors present a pyramid structure for high performance in the world of leadership (Figure I.2).

Figure I.2 This high-performance pyramid is used in leadership training.
Reprinted by permission of Harvard Business School Press. From "The Making of a Corporate Athlete," *Harvard Business Review* 79, by J. Loehr and T. Schwartz. Boston, MA 2001, pp. 120–128. Copyright © 2001 by the Harvard Business School Publishing Corporation.

The base of the pyramid consists of physical capacity. The physical body is the fundamental source of energy. Increasing endurance will lay a foundation for better utilization and management of both emotional and mental capacity. The next level in ascending order is emotional capacity. Regulation of emotions in both oneself and others is one of the most crucial aspects of success and is one of the core aspects of emotional intelligence as defined by Goleman (1995). The next level is mental capacity. Our interpretations of occurrences immediately affect our emotions and behaviors. In other words, the way we think affects the way we act. All humans have patterns of thinking that influence behavior. Some are less than beneficial, and others are even damaging. Changing thinking patterns is a principal component of all major psychological interventions. The final level is spiritual capacity. This refers to the establishment of a value system and the use of this system to guide behavior.

Although the components of the high-performance pyramid have been individually recognized as essential for successful functioning, their inclusion in one model serves as a guide for those interested in improving personal leadership performance. All four components are necessary for success.

This book will focus predominately on the two middle levels of the pyramid, emotional and mental capacity, simply because this is where most of the psychological research applicable to leadership coaching has occurred. The less comprehensive examination of the physical and spiritual capacities in no way discounts their importance. For many leaders, the spiritual capacity might be of higher importance and therefore more interesting than the other capacities. Psychological research, however, has only just begun studying the effects of spiritual capacity on job performance. In regard to physical capacity, research has focused on a very limited set of topics, such as stress management. This also limits the amount of material that can be presented in this text.

Through mastering the potential of the four capacities, you can greatly modify your performance and, in turn, positively affect the performance of the people who work under you.

Figure I.3 demonstrates the combination of the two models.

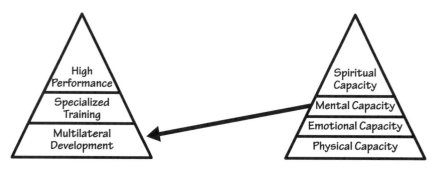

Figure I.3 The two high-performance pyramids can be used together.

The characteristics of the high-performance athletic pyramid are the base of the pyramid leading to high performance in leadership. Gains in physical, mental, emotional, and spiritual capacities comprise the multilateral development of the first triangle. Both models are essential. A leader who does not grow in these capacities will only falter in attempts to reach the level of high-performance leadership. This book therefore is only the beginning of a long, and perhaps challenging and satisfying, journey to high-performance leadership.

Acknowledgements

Numerous individuals made this book possible. However, without the efforts of the following people, this project would not have come to fruition. First, Eric Nei, who edited an encyclopedia-sized manuscript into its present manageable size and who added his own unmistakable identity to the text through the presentation of information about which the author was unaware. Second, Melody Snider, who acquired this book for the ACA, kept the work on track, and honestly expressed her concerns. Third, all of the camp directors I pestered and interviewed during the writing process. Finally, all of the researchers whose work I incorporated into the text.

CHAPTER 1

LEADERSHIP

Overview

The definition of a "leader" is constantly changing. One current conception of leadership looks at the skills of the leader in a specific organization and at his or her interactions with followers. Leaders in small organizations are often required to assume traditional management roles in addition to the duties of a leader, even though these two styles are often at odds with one another. In addition, leaders must assume multiple roles that require different skills in order to be successful. The potential for role conflict, as well as role integration, is greater in small organizations. This book will help the leader or manager of a small organization move toward role integration.

Leadership Defined

The majority of people reading this book are either in leadership positions already or are likely to assume leadership in the near future. But what does it mean to be a leader?

At one time, a leader was considered an individual who was born with a set of specific leadership qualities that set him or her apart from other people. Examples of such qualities include high motivation, tenacity, and organizational skills. A person lacking such inborn qualities could certainly train for leadership and might even find success with the skills. This type of leader, however, would never be able to rival the skills of the "born leader." This conception of inborn leadership was later challenged and found lacking in application to the real world.

The next theory of leadership to develop was referred to as the situational approach. According to this approach, specific situations call for specific types of leadership, and no single type of leadership can be successful across all possible conditions. The availability of resources, the history of the organization, and the nature of the organization's work all affect the leadership skills needed. A dynamic and charismatic leader might be just the right type of person for one organization but could be a highly destructive force in a different facility. This theory suggests that the specifics of the organization dictate the leadership style needed.

The most recent understanding of leadership builds upon the situational model by introducing the presence of followers. Indeed, a leader necessarily requires the presence of followers. The existence of followers is considered a paramount situational factor. Leaders interact with and affect their followers, but the reverse is also true. Followers also interact with and affect their leaders. Followers affect leaders in a more consistent and dynamic fashion than almost all other possible situational factors. If followers do not perceive a formal leader as an effective leader, that leader's influence will be severely curtailed.

Before I define leadership, it is important to first note the differences between a leader and a manager. While many people consider them the same thing, others would argue that they are actually very separate entities. Current texts, for example, are geared for either the manager or the leader, rarely both. We assume that each has a separate role to play in an organization and therefore requires a separate set of skills. The major responsibility of the manager is, of course, to manage. The manager attempts to simplify an organization through tasks such as planning and budgeting, staffing, controlling, creating policy and procedures, and minimizing the effects of change. Management is equated with control of complexity.

Leadership is defined differently. Leaders look for change. They also set a vision for an organization based on the need for change and inspire and motivate employees to move in the desired direction. Leaders set up destabilizing factors in an organization in order to improve it. The most difficult challenge they have is to mobilize the staff to work toward the new goals (all leaders are familiar with staff discontent and resistance to change). Leaders work with managers to administer the change process.

Some individuals are more comfortable and successful in the position of a manager while others feel better in the role of a leader. Management and leadership often require a set of skills that are at cross-purposes with each other. This makes sense because leaders strive to create change while managers strive to minimize the chaotic effects and complexity of change. There are numerous examples of successful leaders and of successful managers, but there are few examples of the combination leader-managers. In large organizations, for example, there is often a clear differentiation between a manager and a leader.

The distinction between leaders and managers is often lost in small work environments such as camps and retreat facilities. In such places, it is common for an individual to be both a leader and a manager. A leader, in addition to setting a vision, may have to assume management activities such as intervening in personnel difficulties, raising money, and meeting with customers. The smaller the business is, the more likely it is to have no concrete division between the two roles.

The Roles of a Leader

In preparation for this book, I interviewed many leaders from different small organizations, including camps and retreat facilities. In each interview, I first asked for a definition of leadership. Many answers were given for this, but after several interviews it became apparent that leaders were not able to give a general definition of the word. Instead, most broke down the role into assorted tasks. Leadership, in their descriptions, consists of numerous skills. Many leaders, for example, described the need for impeccable people skills, others for strong organizational skills, and some for creativity and innovation.

The variety of skills required for leadership, as reported by those interviewed, reflects a commonly understood but little appreciated fact: An abundance of skills is necessary because leaders assume numerous roles in an organization, and the smaller the organization is, the larger the list of necessary skills. Each of the leader's roles involves a different set of abilities. A leader might have to assume the role of disciplinarian in dealing with one disruptive employee, the role of liaison for settling a conflict between two employees, and the role of broadcaster for informing staff of changes in work protocol. Leadership is not simply one role, but rather it is an assortment of numerous roles all grouped under one title and each requiring a specific set of skills.

Henry Mintzberg (1975), in an article titled "The Manager's Job: Folklore and Fact," compiled a thorough list of ten roles a manager must assume. Nine are accurate descriptions of the roles of a leader. These nine roles, described below, reveal that even Mintzberg, with his focus on management, was aware that it is impossible to separate leadership skills from management skills. The tenth role, incidentally, is that of a leader.

- **The figurehead role**—Every leader must perform some ceremonial duties. For example, in a summer camp, the identified leader may be the person who presides over large events or officially opens a camp for the summer season. Other organizations might have the leader greet new employees and give a brief history of the business.

- **The liaison role**—Leaders usually spend as much time with peers and other people outside their own immediate work groups as they do with their own subordinates. The leader might contact people outside the organization for advice or simply to discuss changes occurring in the field. Leaders who attend American Camping Association (ACA) conferences and meet with other professionals are an example of this role.

- **The monitor role**—A good leader is perpetually scanning for information that can affect the organization. A leader who attends a workshop on the most recent advances in the field is an example. Another example is a leader who subscribes to and reads journals or magazines pertinent to the field.

- **The disseminator role**—The leader passes on privileged information to subordinates. A leader who presents information in a staff meeting is an example.

- **The spokesperson role**—This role is filled when a leader sends information to people outside the immediate work group. Almost all leaders must report to somebody, such as a boss, an owner, or a board of directors. When a leader acquires important information in the monitor role, it is up to the leader to present it to those who can use it. As an example, a camp director might have to meet with a board of directors to discuss staff issues occurring in the camp.

- **The entrepreneur role**—After having obtained important information in the role of a monitor, the leader applies the information by changing conditions in the organization. These changes are meant to improve the workings of the agency.

- **The disturbance handler**—This is probably the role leaders are most familiar with. In this role, the leader must cope with an array of problematic situations to maintain the smooth functioning of the organization. For example, a leader acting as a disturbance handler will intervene between two employees whose inability to work together is affecting productivity.

- **The resource allocator**—Here, the leader decides who will get what. Since all organizations have a limited budget, the leader must determine how to allot resources for particular activities, such as money for arts and crafts supplies instead of archery. As a resource allocator, the leader must decide how to portion out the financial, material, and human resources available.

- **The negotiator role**—It is usually the leader who signs the contracts for materials or human resources. In this role, the leader attempts to find an agreement that best fits the organization. Attempting to negotiate a raise for employees and, at the same time, maintaining fiscal health is an example.

All of these roles are interrelated, and most problems in an organization require the coordination of several roles. The following examples show how some leaders have combined the many leadership roles as they carry out their responsibilities.

Example

David is the manager of a residential retreat facility. In the summer it is used as a camp and in the winter as a conference center. In attending a camp conference (**liaison role**), he hears that several other retreats in the area are having problems with the presence of bears (**monitor role**). David knows that during the summer there was one bear sighting at his facility, but no other bear-related problems. David contacts the local nature center and finds that bears are indeed becoming much more of a presence in the area and a possible threat (**monitor role**). He also learns that a small housing development is being constructed on a private forested area several miles from his facility, which could well increase the presence of bears on his own property (**monitor role**). David writes a letter of concern to the board of directors of his facility (**spokesperson role**) in which he explains his concerns and offers concrete suggestions for reducing the possible threat (**entrepreneur role**). Upon approval of his suggestions, David informs his staff of the changes in working protocol (**disseminator role**).

Example

Darlene, the director of a summer camp, is alarmed to find that one of the most problematic children from the previous summer—a relative of one of the board members—has been signed up to return for the upcoming season (**monitor role**). She informs the supervisor of the boys' camp (**disseminator role**) and requests input from him about how to handle the child (**monitor role** and a proactive **disturbance handler**). To permit the youth to return would jeopardize the smooth operation of the program, but to refuse his admittance would be politically risky. Darlene contacts several peers for their advice (**liaison role**). They decide to issue a precamp agreement focusing on appropriate and inappropriate behaviors (**entrepreneur role**). Darlene, as the director, takes it upon herself to approach the particular board member about the dilemma and proposed solution (**spokesperson role**). Since Darlene sincerely wants the boy to have a positive experience at camp, she offers to place him with one of the most experienced counselors (**resource allocator role**). Darlene and the board member discuss the problem and agree on the solution (**negotiator role**).

If you lead a small organization, you have probably been in each of these roles. And as if these roles weren't enough work, leaders usually assume other roles that have nothing to do with work, such as parenting and volunteering. If you are one of these leaders, you will be happy to learn that in the field of psychology successfully accomplishing the tasks of numerous roles is considered a sign of stability. There is also evidence that an increase in the number of roles taken on by a person results in an increase in energy to perform such multiple roles. Altogether, the numerous work–and nonwork–related roles assumed by a leader are emotionally and intellectually positive. Leaders can congratulate themselves on their mental health.

There is, however, the unfortunate fact that role conflict is inevitable. There is eventually a point where a leader must perform too many roles at the same time. A leader has only so much time and so much energy, and the stress of numerous roles can negatively affect performance. There is no formula for the number of roles that a person can take on successfully. It depends on the abilities of each individual leader. I'll address this topic later in the book.

Another Role

One fundamental belief underlying this book is that leaders powerfully affect the performance of the people who work under them. This is strongly supported by psychological and organizational research (Goleman, Boyatzis, and McKee, 2002). One of the most important–and for many employees, *the* most important–factors in job satisfaction is their relationship with their immediate supervisor. Satisfied employees positively affect productivity and increase the overall satisfaction of the leader in his or her position.

In our previous list of leadership roles, one was neglected. Mintzberg may not have seen this role if much of his research was done in large corporations. In smaller organizations, however, it is common. This is the **support role**. Small facilities allow for a much closer relationship among employees; people know what is going on with one another both inside and outside of the job. One woman who was interviewed, for example, reported that she was well aware of the difficulties that her eight staff members were experiencing at home including medical, financial, and family problems. Staff members in small facilities will come to a leader to discuss important events not necessarily related to work. Having to assume many roles while, at the same time, having personal contact with staff presents challenges for leaders of small facilities.

This book will assist the leader in understanding and augmenting the skills necessary for leadership. It cannot be overemphasized that if a leader has the physical, emotional, mental, and spiritual capacities necessary for leadership, he or she will positively affect the performance of subordinates who will in turn bolster the skills of the leader. All of this results in a strongly functioning organization.

Summary of Key Points

1. Leadership is not based on inborn qualities but is rather a set of skills necessary for a specific work environment and for successful interactions with followers (subordinates).

2. Leaders will definitely affect the performance of followers. Followers will also affect the performance of the leader. Successful skills in interacting with and managing other people are some of the most crucial requirements of leadership.

3. Managers attempt to create stability in organizations through tasks such as budgeting, hiring, creating policies and procedures, and reducing the effects of change.

4. Leaders look for change, set a vision for an organization based on the need for change, and inspire and motivate employees to move in the desired direction. Leaders set up destabilizing factors in order to improve the organization.

5. Leaders in small organizations must often assume the roles of both leader and manager even though the goals of each role are often at cross-purposes.

6. Leaders, in addition, have many other goals to assume, including figurehead, liaison, monitor, disseminator. spokesperson, entrepreneur, disturbance handler, resource allocator, negotiator, and support person.

7. Conflicting leadership roles can affect the leader's performance and potential.

8. Conflicting leadership roles can be more of a problem in small organizations because of the personal relationships that develop among staff and leaders.

CHAPTER 2

THE BASIC FOUR

Overview

The recognition of four internal experiences is necessary for successful leadership: thoughts, feelings, sensations, and impulses. Thoughts are the easiest to recognize in oneself. People have varying ability to recognize the other three. Leaders can and must teach themselves to recognize all of their own internal stimuli.

The Four Components of Experience

The more science explores the workings of the human body, the more apparent its complexity becomes. Even the simplest of occurrences, such as recognizing a friend on the street or feeling a sense of annoyance, requires hundreds—if not thousands—of interconnected and coordinated responses inside the body. It is certainly far easier to observe how a person behaves externally, but external behavior is ultimately the end result of hidden internal events. A person who has misplaced his keys, for example, would demonstrate several outward responses, such as a look of annoyance or anger, rapid movements around the immediate environment as he attempts to find the keys, and mumbled words as he tries to recall the last place the keys were placed. These responses, no matter how dramatic they may appear, pale in comparison to what is occurring inside his body. Hormones flood the body. Neurotransmitters activate the brain. Fine and gross motor movements prime the muscles. Heart rate, temperature, and respiration change. The internal reactions to an external event, such as lost keys, can number in the thousands.

Are humans aware of all of these changes? With some medical conditions, the answer is *yes*. Diabetics, for example, learn to recognize even mild changes in glucose levels that a nondiabetic would be completely unaware of. However, most of us are unaware of internal fluctuations. We can be thankful for this, for if we had to monitor every single change that takes place within the body, it would be impossible to function. Imagine if we had life-sustaining functions under conscious control. Remembering to keep our hearts beating might require so much attention that there would be little time for any other activity. In general, knowledge of internal changes would complicate our daily life.

There are, however, some internal experiences that are well worth becoming acquainted with. Four particular internal occurrences are referenced throughout this book. None will be new since they are all common experiences. Some occur on a moment-to-moment basis, and others occur at least several times per day. These four consist of emotions, thoughts, sensations, and impulses. Sensations refer to the recognition of the actual physical reactions that occur within the body. For example, if a person has a cold, the accompanying physical sensations include lethargy, congestion, and probably headache. If a person experiences anger, probable related sensations include a feeling of warmth and a noticeable increase in the heart rate. Anxiety causes the well-known sensation of butterflies in the stomach.

Impulses are an immediate desire to act. For example, a person who is cut off while driving might have the immediate desire to honk the horn. A person who is reprimanded by her boss might have the immediate urge to strike back verbally or physically, or she may decide with little reflection to quit her job. Impulses are immediate, instinctive, or learned reactions that may or may not be constructive responses to external events. Fortunately most people do not act on impulse; otherwise life would be far more complicated than it already is.

Impulse control has been a subject of increasing interest in the past decade due to new studies of the brain. Two findings are particularly important. First, it appears that some people are born with less impulse control than others. It is considered part of their inborn temperament. These people will likely struggle with impulse problems their lifetime through, although the consequences can be reduced through specific training. Second, current research shows that impulse control matures along with physical maturity. Development of the brain affects impulse control, which does not fully develop until the mid-twenties. (There appears to be no decline in impulse control unless there is a decline in cognitive ability, such as from a brain disorder that can occur as part of the aging process.)

This research is important for leaders who manage younger staff. Staff members in their late teens or early twenties, while certainly exhibiting more impulse management than children and young teenagers, have not yet mastered impulse control. This does not devalue the employment of younger people. It does inform the leader about the physiological limitations that may change the expectations of a young staff.

Thoughts and Emotions

Most people can easily recognize their thoughts. There is more variation in recognizing sensations, impulses, and emotions. One major reason for this is that the traditional education system has been focused on cognitive development. More and more educators realize the necessity of focusing on emotional development, but most do not know how to implement successful programs.

There are other reasons for variations in self-awareness. The ability to recognize internal stimuli, called introspection, is another characteristic of inborn temperament. There are those who are naturally introspective and those who are not, although those who are not born with this temperament can certainly develop it through training and practice. Regarding emotions specifically, females tend to be more aware of their emotions than males; female brains are "wired" for better self-knowledge of their emotional states. Males can have further difficulties in that they are socialized to express a limited emotional range, which is usually limited to broad feelings of "good," "bad," and "angry."

In general, people who are more introspective are better able to label their feelings; they have a rich emotional vocabulary. Those who lack a rich emotional vocabulary can often frustrate those who are emotionally aware. One highly introspective camp leader complained that, after firing a popular staff member, he was only able to elicit feelings of "bad" and "okay" from his remaining male staff members. These two emotions did not begin to match his own feelings or his guesses as to what his staff members were feeling. His staff members did have feelings about the firing, but they either did not have labels for their feelings or they felt uncomfortable expressing themselves more profoundly.

Increasing emotional vocabulary can result in increased awareness. To say that you are mad does not offer much information. Is it fury? Rage? Minor annoyance? All of these are derivations of anger but offer much more information. A leader would certainly respond differently to someone who is annoyed than to someone who is enraged. Yet many people would use "mad" to express this very complicated emotional state.

Summary of Key Points

1. The human body demonstrates both internal and external reactions to daily occurrences.

2. The visible external reactions are minimal compared to the hundreds—if not thousands—of internal reactions.

3. The four most important internal reactions for leadership development are thoughts, feelings, sensations, and impulses.

4. Most people are aware of their thoughts, but there is great variation in insight into the other three internal experiences.

5. A purposeful increase in monitoring for these internal events will result in more self-control and better leadership.

CHAPTER 3

PHYSICAL CAPACITY

If activity is understood as unnatural and not part of everyday life, there is a concomitant sense that occasional or sporadic activity suffices. One has met one's obligation. The absurdity of this perspective can be understood by examining parallel assumptions regarding other natural aspects of being. For example, do we object to sleep at night? Do we plan to stock up on sleep so that we won't need to do it again? Do we say, "If I get 8 hours of sleep for 2 weeks, then I'll be perfectly rested for the next 3 months"? (Hays, p. 9)

Overview

Physical capacity composes the base of the high-performance pyramid. While a leader may already have very good emotional and mental capacities, without a strong physical capacity, his or her use of these abilities will not likely be maximized. The core ingredients of high physical capacity consist of diet, physical activity, stress management, and rest. Each leader must devise his or her own strategy for maximizing physical capacity. Achieving a fitness lifestyle can be very easy or very difficult.

The Benefits of Increased Physical Capacity

The creators of the high-performance pyramid believe that physical capacity is the core necessity for success. Others, however, question this assumption. This book assumes that all levels of the pyramid are equally important. At times, one capacity will be called upon more than the others will. In such circumstances, if a leader is lacking in a certain capacity he or she will come up short in that situation.

While you can certainly make use of emotional and mental capacities without partaking in any effort to increase physical aptitude, there is every reason to doubt that you will maximize your efficiency. Fortunately, obtaining the minimum physical capacity is not difficult. Due to the many roles and challenges that leadership jobs entail, most leaders will find themselves striving for more than just the minimum.

Several of the reasons for augmenting physical capacity are as follows.

- **Increased self-esteem**—Since humans can pay attention to only a limited number of details, a person who does not need to be concerned with appearance or health problems necessarily has more time to attend to other leader-related involvements. In addition, high self-esteem will improve one's interactions with other people.

- **Improved health**—Through involvement in a fitness lifestyle, you will improve your health. This can be seen in increased resistance to illness, resiliency after injuries and infections, and decreased absenteeism from work due to illness.

- **Increased vigor and endurance**—Leadership is an endless series of challenges. Exhaustion, fatigue, and an inability to bounce back from setbacks can occur for a leader who has not developed a fitness lifestyle. An increase in physical capacity will enable the leader to meet the demands of the position without damaging health effects or crippling burnout.

Unfortunately, there is much questionable (and sometimes harmful) information available regarding increased physical capacity. Even in a world awash with information, people still make bad decisions about their own health. Consider the following examples.

- The diet industry is a multibillion-dollar industry to which people keep returning again and again in spite of repeated failures. Furthermore, no diet has ever been shown to keep weight off except for a very small number of individuals.

- Eating plans involving low carbohydrates or low protein continue to recycle in spite of questionable health benefits.

- Steroids have become more frequently used by both males and females for sports improvement in spite of known damaging health effects.

- Many confuse body weight and body composition. They believe that lost weight is the sign of progress when, in reality, how that weight is lost (fluid, muscle, fat) determines the detriment or benefit of that weight loss.

It is important to carefully evaluate sources of information regarding health and fitness. Two of the big sources are as follows.

- **Sales and advertising**—In 1951 the Relax-A-Cizor was introduced. It was one of the first products offered for mainstream, mass-consumption health improvement. It promised to change body weight and shape without exercise or diet modifications. You only had to lie on the machine (even nap, if desired) and allow electric charges to stimulate your muscles. The Food and Drug Administration officially banned it in 1966, not only because it did nothing, but also because the electrical current could cause heart damage. Since then, there have been thousands of machines (including electrical devices that target specific muscle groups), supplements, and diets that purportedly benefit health. Newspapers, magazines, television shows, and even in-store product demonstrations promise that the users of this device or that supplement will acquire health and physical perfection. Some of the products really do have benefit. Others do not. The goal of such products is to make money for their parent companies. It is up to the buyer to evaluate the validity of fitness products and plans.

- **Other people**—While this may sound contradictory, a person who has obtained apparent fitness may be a bad source of information. Think of a friend who strongly recommended a diet. How long did he or she keep the weight off? Recall bodybuilders who admitted, at the end of their careers, that steroid use had been a major factor in their fitness program. I remember one muscle-bound gentleman who taught his "simple exercise techniques" to a group of high school athletes. Much later the students found that this man had been less than honest. He actually worked out seven days per week for four hours each day! As will become evident throughout this book, each person is both enabled or limited by genetics. The buffed individual at the gym may simply have inherited genes that make his buffed body more easily attainable.

There are many ways to increase physical capacity. Some work, and some do not work. The following section will begin an exploration of the proven components of increasing this essential capacity.

A Fitness Lifestyle

There is no longer any mystery about how to achieve physical fitness. The necessary information is everywhere, including on the side panel of many cereal boxes. However, many people desire more than just fitness. In a society that focuses so much attention on the perfect physical body, many individuals seek an idealized body. Unfortunately, a general fitness lifestyle will likely not result in a perfect physique.

Hawley and Burke write about the differences between athletic performance and general fitness. "While both are worthy causes, the athlete strives to extend the barriers of human capability through severe, fatigue-inducing training sessions...On the other hand, most, if not all, of the health-related benefits of regular exercise can be realized by most individuals through a more moderate approach to physical activity" (p. 34).

Nowhere in these definitions does it state that fitness includes physical beauty and bodily perfection. If you are seeking general fitness, you will find readily available information sufficient. Specifically, you will find that physical fitness involves eating healthy foods, exercising, managing stress, and getting ample rest.

You should identify a goal before beginning a physical fitness lifestyle. Is it to simply increase health and energy? The requirements are rather easy to incorporate into the daily routine. Is your goal to improve specific sports-related skills such as for basketball or wrestling? You must take a different approach that will require much more energy, time, and perseverance. If your goal is to look your best, you must take yet another approach. It is, of course, possible to have any combination of the above goals, such as a desire for excellence in a particular sport, for looking your best, and for being healthy at the same time.

There is much controversy over the goal of looking your best, and there are numerous examples of how a focus on only this goal can lead to serious negative consequences. For example, over the last decade, many teenagers have begun using steroids to add muscle, improve athletic performance, increase the personal feeling of self-satisfaction, and in many cases add to their attractiveness in the eyes of others. This is the short-term pursuit of physical perfection and social admiration at the cost of long-term health and happiness, because the long-term risks (not to mention the short-term risks) of steroid use are tremendous.

Many researchers and writers in the field decry the focus of a fitness lifestyle for the mere sake of cosmetic change. They believe that by using slender models for everything from soap powder to jewelry, the media set up an impossible ideal of physical perfection, which leads viewers to feel dissatisfied with their own bodies. Other writers ignore media influence completely and even perpetuate the myth that physical perfection is a natural desire—a mere fact of life. In light of this information and misinformation, you must set your own goal(s) that are appropriate for your general lifestyle and genetic makeup. Physically fit individuals will have more energy, suffer fewer injuries and illnesses, and have a more positive outlook on life. If you have an additional desire to work on athletic improvement and physical perfection, then go for it. It is only when these two latter goals begin to interfere with improved physical health that they might become problems.

The following pages will focus on the four components of a fitness lifestyle: an eating plan, exercise, stress management, and rest.

Eating Plan

Diet can be defined in two ways. The first diet is a process of losing weight. The second diet is the usual foods eaten by a person. In both cases, diet affects physical performance. In addition, the food you eat will influence emotional and mental capacities. For example, a person who eats a low-calorie diet for weight-loss purposes may experience fatigue, poor concentration, and erratic mood swings.

Consider the following facts about eating and dieting. At any one time, approximately twenty-five percent of men and forty-five percent of women are attempting to lose weight. Americans spend more than 33 billion dollars per year on weight-loss products and services. Liposuction is now the leading form of cosmetic surgery. Diet books top the bestseller lists. Genetic researchers are looking for genes responsible for obesity in hopes of formulating some intervention to affect weight. Even biotechnology firms are attempting to create food products that do not add weight, such as the fat substitute olestra used in popular snack foods. Clearly, weight is a concern at the personal and corporate level.

The camping industry is also concerned with weight. Camps that incorporate, or have as their primary focus, a component of better living through physical activity are common. Some camps focus exclusively on changing eating habits and weight. Attendance at such camps is consistently high. Some people argue that weight-loss camps are gouging our pocketbooks for the sake of personal profit. While this may be true of other corporations and institutions, it certainly is not true of camps since the cumulative effects of the camp experience on youths and families is positive. While a child may or may not lose weight at a camp, the positive effects of camping are well founded. At a minimum, camp is a place where children and adults will be more physically active than in their regular routine.

In this country, more than half of all adults are considered overweight (ten to thirty percent above an "ideal" weight). Therefore, it is not surprising that one of the most common strategies for achieving self-satisfaction is weight loss.

The effects of carrying excess weight are not often pronounced, but they are real. One study found that overweight females completed fewer years of school and had lower household incomes in comparison to average weight individuals. The likely causes for such findings are societal and psychological rather than physical. Thinness is the accepted cultural norm in the United States. Americans believe that they can effortlessly achieve physical perfection. Failure to do so brings disappointment and depression.

Because weight is believed to be controllable, overweight people are often considered to lack self-control. People may hold negative prejudices about an overweight individual and may demonstrate a lack of respect for her based solely on physical appearance. Therefore excess weight can not only affect a leader's self-satisfaction but may also elicit negative reactions from other people. This is a particular problem for a camp leader since the position is typically very visible and very public.

For individuals who are obese (thirty to one hundred percent above an "ideal" weight), the physical challenges of carrying so much weight can directly affect stamina and performance. Let's discuss what is known about weight. Decades ago, four million people who were insured by life insurance companies in the United States were weighed and measured. These figures were used to create a formula for an ideal correlation between weight and height and life expectancy. In theory, an ideal weight reduced health complications and increased life span. While this formula is now an accepted part of American health care, it has numerous flaws and is increasingly shown to be of negligible value.

A problem with this formula is that it does not consider the natural distribution of weight among people of the same height. Some six-foot-tall males are heavier than their ideal weight simply because they overeat and do not exercise. Others weigh above the same ideal because of a naturally slower metabolism or inborn predisposition to have more fat deposits. People have many different shapes and sizes because each individual has a built-in control system dictating the body's percentage of fat. Many people are genetically programmed to be heavier. Studies of identical twins showed that if one twin was obese, his or her twin was likely to also be obese. In an attempt to rule out the role of a shared environment, other studies looked at twins who were separated and raised by adoptive families. These studies showed that there was no relationship between the weight of the twins and the weight of their adoptive families, yet obesity still occurred in both twins. Similarly, studies of families over many generations indicate that the location of fat on the body is inheritable.

Another interesting genetic link to weight comes from the number of taste buds on the tongue. In fact, one gene regulates the number of taste buds. Some individuals have 1,100 taste buds per square centimeter on the tongue, while others have a meager 11 in the same area. Those who have a higher number are particularly sensitive to the taste and temperature of food. They also tend to be thinner individuals. Those with fewer taste buds can eat just about anything and tend to weigh more. Thus, a person's sensitivity to food, stemming from one gene, affects the amount of food eaten.

The theories of ideal weight have provoked great controversy over the health effects that come with being overweight. For men and women who have no pre-existing health problems associated with their weight, life expectancy will not improve with weight loss. It is still unclear if the recognized effects of moderate weight loss (improvement in hypertension, lipid levels, and insulin secretion) are even long-standing. However, it does appear that for those who are experiencing health problems associated with weight, a loss does increase the lifespan as well as vitality.

To further complicate this matter, the process of losing weight may even be harmful. It is a fact that ninety percent of people who diet to lose weight will regain it and will add several pounds in the process. No diet has been found to keep weight off more than a small fraction of dieters. Researchers are questioning whether permanent weight loss is even possible. Thus individuals begin to cycle through diets; they lose weight, regain it, and then restart the process. Research indicates that this cycle can result in coronary heart disease and consequently decrease life expectancy. In addition, each time a person begins yet another weight-loss attempt, it will be more difficult than the time before. Repeated dieting attempts make the body more resistant to future weight loss.

Finally, a gradual weight gain throughout the middle-age years of life seems normal. In fact, individuals who gradually gain weight during middle age have fewer health risks than those who do not gain weight.

As stated earlier, this book will not tell you what goal to set regarding your fitness lifestyle, but, armed with the most current information, you may decide that sustained weight loss is possible and will improve self-esteem, increase confidence in relationships, and augment leadership capability. But keep in mind that almost all people who diet without making permanent changes in lifestyle will regain their weight and risk possible long-term health consequences. A focus on weight alone, without giving attention to the other components of being well (exercise and rest), will very likely result in a temporary, cosmetic change only.

One way to lose weight is through dehydration. This method is, at best, short-term and dangerous. It can lead to headaches, impaired physical co-ordination and endurance, and consumption of nonnutritious food and drinks. Another way to lose weight is to lose lean muscle. Unless you are discontinuing your career as a competitive body builder, there is little benefit in this. That leaves only one healthful and helpful option: Reduce your percentage of body fat. Let's look at this option.

Fat loss is the best method of weight loss. Before we examine this topic, we need to refute a common perception. Most people measure weight loss in terms of pounds. ("I lost seven pounds in the past two weeks.") In fact, weight is a very poor measurement of progress. Recalling the information about weight loss and dehydration, if we knew that a person had lost four pounds in fluid we might actually begin to feel concern for that individual's health. The loss of fluids or muscle tissue might seem like progress on the bathroom scale, but they are a setup for poor health and future weight gain. Individuals who exercise may actually see weight gains as more muscle is formed. This is not a sign of failure but of progress. A good general rule is not to attempt to lose actual pounds of weight but rather to gain muscle and lose fat as a percentage of body weight. The more muscle tissue you have the higher your metabolic rate will be because lean muscle tissue burns more calories than fat tissue even when you are sitting still.

In addition, lean muscle tends to be denser than fat. In other words, a pound of lean muscle will take up less space than a pound of fat. Therefore, people may actually maintain their weight while trimming their waistline.

Many diets achieve their apparent success from the loss of lean muscle tissue, the one tissue that can make a difference in weight maintenance when the diet ends. If you are contemplating a diet, have a body composition analysis performed (a relatively cheap and painless procedure now performed at many health clubs) in order to monitor changes in body composition. If you do not want to get a body composition analysis completed, there are other ways to monitor your progress. Your chosen exercise should become more comfortable over time provided you do not increase your intensity. Your clothes should begin to fit better, especially around the waist, buttocks, and thighs. These are signs that you are adjusting your body composition, increasing your lean muscle mass, and decreasing your body fat.

The components of healthy eating are the same for people who are dieting and those who are not. These principles are well known and require little explanation.

- Eat a variety of foods.
- Choose a diet low in salt.
- Choose a diet moderate in sugars.
- Drink alcoholic beverages in moderation or abstain altogether.
- Choose a diet low in saturated fats.
- Choose a diet containing plenty of grain products, fruits, and vegetables.
- Favor lean meat.
- Favor foods that have been minimally processed.
- Drink plenty of low-caffeine, low-sugar fluids.

Those who are making dietary changes as part of an effort to improve body composition (e.g., more muscle and less fat) should keep the following suggestions in mind.

- Choose sensible portion sizes.
- Eat at least five small meals per day rather than three large meals. When you go a long time between meals, your body learns to conserve fat more efficiently. This is probably a trait passed on from our ancestors that assisted in their survival through famines. In spite of its contradictory nature, a person must eat frequently, though in relatively small portions, to lose weight. Through the ingestion of at least five meals per day, blood sugar and insulin levels will be controlled (thus maintaining energy level), protein will be available for growth, and fat will not be stored by the body.
- Don't skip breakfast.
- Eat a breakfast that contributes to the overall daily balance of protein, carbohydrates, and fat.
- Create each meal with approximately one part fat, two parts protein, and three parts carbohydrates. Do not eliminate fat from the diet, as it is essential for good health. Choose unsaturated fats over saturated ones. Protein is necessary for growth and recovery of muscle tissue.
- Adjust carbohydrate intake according to upcoming activity level. A

person who is planning a sedentary activity for the next several hours will require fewer carbohydrates than she would prior to a workout.

- Do not eat based on activities already performed unless you are experiencing unreasonable fatigue following significant physical activity. In this case, your body may need an extra dose of nutritious calories to recover.

- Burn more calories than you take in. To help with this, recall the earlier suggestion of eating five meals per day. Small balanced meals will not only decrease hunger but also assist in weight loss.

- Accept your genetic design. Many individuals are genetically geared to be heavier than what they have come to believe is their ideal weight! Average weight for height is just that—average.

- If, after your best efforts, you are still carrying a few extra pounds, then decide to let that be OK. Do not mourn the body you were never meant to have, but rather feel good about the positive changes you are making.

The role of physical exercise is becoming more recognized in the controversy over dieting and weight loss. Most people know that exercise is healthy. Most people don't know that many of the problems once thought to stem from excess weight may actually be the result of limited physical activity. While there is inconclusive evidence that weight loss affects the life span for healthy people, there is ample evidence that moderate exercise can make a significant health improvement

Making changes in your eating plan can be challenging in a leadership position and especially as a leader in the camping profession. One day you may be at a business lunch courting a potential financial backer. The next day you may be on the road recruiting staff. The next day you may be at the dining hall eating camp food with the visiting school group. And on the next day, you may be too busy to begin with breakfast, stop for lunch, or enjoy any sort of a relaxed supper. Clearly, your challenges are well defined. However, if you have mastered the information so far in this chapter, your response is also well defined. Know yourself and accept your genetic gifts. Set some reasonable goals that are based on what is healthy for you. Ignore popular media images of the ideal body. Finally, remember that your physical capacity is defined more by your body composition than by your weight. With these things in mind, you're ready to meet the challenges of eating well while leading in the camping industry.

Physical Activity

Physical activity does not necessarily mean a formal exercise program. The federal government recommends moderate physical activity of at least one hour a day for adults. Moderate physical activity is defined as the use of energy equal to walking two miles in thirty minutes. This can include everyday activities, such as gardening, raking leaves, climbing stairs, playing with children, and cleaning the house. These activities do not even need to occur in a single chunk of time. If you perform three ten-minute periods of moderate physical exercise throughout the day, you have met the recommended minimum. This is the minimum, though.

A popular program in Japan demonstrates this principle. The program is called 10,000 Steps and the central principle is that some time in the day the average person needs to walk for only a half-hour (all at once or in chunks) in addition to regular daily activities to reach the cumulative daily-recommended 10,000 steps. This prescriptive dose of exercise is not only very achievable and very natural, it is the minimum necessary to reach general physical well-being.

The psychological benefits of physical activity are less well known than the physical benefits, although a mind-body connection is becoming increasingly apparent. Physical activity can increase emotional and cognitive abilities. The following is a list of just some of the psychological effects of an ongoing exercise routine: decrease in depression and anxiety; improved self-concept, mastery, and self-efficacy; and a likely increase in an optimistic outlook on life.

The recognition of physical activity as the catalyst for mental and emotional well-being is not a new concept. In ancient Greece, adults, children, and even the elderly spent hours of each day in exercise.

Exercise improves stress tolerance. Stress affects the body and the mind. At present, it appears as if exercise has a more positive effect on the psychological symptoms associated with stress than on physical symptoms. However, there is no doubt that a combination of physical exercise and other stress-management techniques, such as meditation, can be quite beneficial.

Unfortunately, statistics show that while individuals know the benefits of exercise, many of these same people are not embracing physical activity. The participation in physical activity greatly decreases after the teenage years. Sixty-five percent of adolescents between the ages of ten and seventeen are at least moderately active. Only fifteen percent of adults between the ages of eighteen and sixty-four participate in moderate activity. There are several reasons for a decrease in physical activity. First, we generally do not hunt, gather, or grow the food we eat. In the past, feeding ourselves required the expenditure of huge amounts of calories. Now feeding ourselves is a sedentary activity. Second, we have come to associate leisure with inactivity. Most people imagine vacations in which they will be required to do little, if anything, except lie on the beach. We believe that since we work hard enough at our jobs, we certainly do not want to put out more effort during times of vacation. If you are a person who finds physical activity unappealing, don't forget that the use of physical energy will cause an increase in physical energy. The less energy you use, the less you will have. The more physically active you are, the more energy you will have each and every day.

Third, experience shows that as your role in the camping profession changes from direct program delivery to management, and then to administration, your job will include more sedentary tasks.

For those individuals who desire more than just basic fitness, an exercise regimen is a wonderful option. Exercise is defined as the intentional involvement in physical activity beyond that required for daily living and general fitness. It is specifically designed to move a person to higher levels of physical performance. Individuals and their exercise involvement can be placed into several subcategories.

- **Nonexercisers**—These individuals are the most sedentary, do not currently exercise, and may actively avoid physical activity.
- **Occasional exercisers**—These individuals may exercise occasionally. They usually recognize the benefits of exercise but either cannot or will not maintain ongoing and consistent involvement.
- **Committed exercisers**—These folks have a consistent involvement in exercise and perform their exercise routine at least three times per week.
- **Amateur athletes**—These individuals choose to devote a large part of their discretionary time to athletic pursuits in an effort to gain a competitive edge.
- **Professional athletes**—These individuals exercise for a living. Failure to focus daily on an exercise routine that increases all aspects of physical function will result in a loss of income.

Physically inactive and occasional exercisers have the most to gain by involvement in an exercise regimen. But at all levels of activity, if you are not satisfied with the results of your exercise, you will need to make changes. These may be changes in duration, intensity, or chosen activity.

Keep in mind that genetics plays a major role in muscle development. In most cases, you will never obtain the physique and performance of an athletic hero in spite of your exercise routine. You will be happier if you accept your genetic blueprint for what it is and set your goals within those limits and abilities.

Exercise is generally divided into four categories.

1. **Flexibility training**—This is the ability to move joints and use muscles through their full range of motion. Regular moderate stretching, yoga, and sports that utilize a full range of motion tend to enhance flexibility.

2. **Muscle endurance**—This is the ability of a muscle (or groups of muscles) to continue performance over a period of time. An apt example of this is an individual who can perform increasing repetitions with the same amount of weight with continued practice.

3. **Muscle strength**—This is the ability of a muscle to exert force for a brief period of time. With this type of exercise, an individual can lift increasing amounts of weight as training progresses.

4. **Aerobic training**—This is the ability to deliver oxygen and energy to tissue for an extended period of time.

There are several principles to consider in defining your best exercise protocol.

- **Individual differences**—Every person has different genetic blueprints that will affect exercise results. Several people beginning the exact same exercise routine will have different results. Only some people have the ability to reach the professional athlete status.

- **Use and disuse**—This is also known as "use it or lose it." When you stop your exercise involvement, the accrued benefits will disappear. In addition, it takes much less time to lose these benefits to strength, endurance, flexibility, and cardiovascular health than it did to gain them.

- **Specificity**—Specific results are related to specific training. If you train for strength, you will get stronger. If you spend an hour each day in flexibility training, you will become more flexible, not stronger.

- **Overload**—In order for your body to improve, you must make higher than normal demands on it. If you expend the same amount of effort at each exercise session, you will attain and then remain at that level without greater overload (also called intensity). At the same time, increasing the level of overload too quickly can be discouraging and hurtful. You must find your balance.

- **Progression**—In order for your body to adapt, it must be continually challenged. There must be a gradual but consistent increase in the work your body performs whether it be, for example, adding more weight or running for a longer time.

The overload and progression principles are particularly important. A woman who decides to begin riding her bike three miles a day to her job will begin to experience the benefits of physical exercise. The activity will increase her cardiovascular activity, flexibility, strength, and endurance. After a short time, however, she will have reached a plateau. Though she might be feeling great, her ability to go above this level will be limited. If, for example, she decides to participate in a ten-mile bike race, she might find herself unable to continue after the first several miles of the race. Her body had adapted to the three-mile commute but was not ready for more than that. To better prepare herself for the race she should gradually add additional mileage to the daily commute until she reaches the ten-mile capacity. If she then wants to cover that distance at a faster time, she will need to practice riding faster. Through this method, she will be gradually overloading her body and encouraging it to adapt to a higher level of physical activity.

Another example is a gentleman who wants to develop his chest muscles. In a screening for exercise, he finds that he can bench press eighty pounds five times before exhaustion. He does not like the gym and decides to exercise at home. He begins to do push-ups every day. This will result in increased strength and endurance. At the next screening several weeks later, he can perform ten presses with eighty-five pounds. This definitely indicates a strength increase. This is where the problem comes in. Though our man may be able to perform more and more push-ups on a daily basis, each time he returns to the gym he will still only be able to lift the eighty-five pounds. Why isn't he getting any stronger? In reality, he is increasing his muscle endurance through the push-ups. Strength increases require lifting more weight. Yet he is lifting the same weight, his own body, for more repetitions only. If he were to ask his forty-pound daughter to sit on his back every time he did his push-ups, the number of repetitions would drop dramatically but his strength would increase, and the next time he tested himself with a bench press, he would be able to lift more weight. This man was training specifically for endurance even though he may have wanted more strength. His body progressed to the strength level at which it could lift its own weight but would not increase further until he overloaded it by adding more weight.

The final principle of physical activity is variety. Variety encourages you to change the exercises you normally perform. Through the addition of more weight or the complete change of activity, your body will be encouraged to adapt. Add variety to the program. With a basic understanding of the different types of exercise and the principles that underlie success, let's examine what would constitute a good exercise program. Remember, though, exercise is not essential. If you are satisfied with your body, maintain good health, and perform moderate physical activity daily, you do not need to go out and exercise. An increase in moderate physical activity for sixty minutes daily is enough to benefit health. Just keep in mind that the same principles apply for physical activity as for exercise; the body will adapt to a specific level unless overload and progression occur.

As with an eating plan, it is first important to know your goals. If you want to run a marathon, establish an exercise that focuses on building your aerobic capacity. Add to this some flexibility exercises to prevent injury. Then add a little strength training to improve running efficiency and overall strength. Conversely, if your sport of choice involves sudden but short bursts of speed or matching of one person's strength against another, such as in contact sports, you will need to focus on strength training. Begin with weight lifting that includes few repetitions per set before muscle fatigue. Then add some flexibility training to prevent injury and to maintain or improve range of motion. Then add some aerobic training to improve your ability to sustain effort over time. The principle is, match your training to your goals.

However, if your goal is increased fitness and toning of the body, include all aspects of exercise in a regimen (aerobic, strength, endurance, and flexibility). None of these areas should dominate your routine. Virtually everything you do on a daily basis needs only a minimum of aerobic endurance. Twenty to thirty minutes of aerobic exercise three times per week is sufficient for most daily activity. Muscle development speeds up metabolism; the more muscle you have, the more calories you will use every day, even in sedentary states. In addition, the trunk muscles (hips to neck, not including the arms) contribute significantly to good posture, efficient movement, and the daily physical requirements of bending, lifting, and sitting. Focus on a muscle development routine that develops these muscles to improve your daily routine endurance. Finally, good flexibility promotes good movement and prevents injury. In addition, flexibility tends to be the first physical ability affected by the aging process. As you can see, the best exercise program depends on your goals. If your goal is improved physical well-being in general, then an exercise program focusing on the development of lean muscle tissue with supplementary flexibility and aerobic involvement is your best bet.

Now, let's imagine that you have decided to be more physically active. You now see, or perhaps you were reminded, that including physical activity in your life will help you be healthier and happier and a better camp professional. You get the idea. If you have any doubts about safely implementing the principles in this chapter because of your age, health history, or current physical condition, see your family physician. As a team, you can safely improve your leadership capacity by focusing on your physical capacity.

Stress Management

Entire industries have been built around the topic of stress management. In spite of the apparent complexity surrounding the concept, stress can be recognized easily. Stress is defined as the physical and psychological effects stemming from demands on an individual that exceed his or her present coping ability.

Stress can be divided into several categories. The first is short-term stress as compared to long-term stress. Precamp training is a short-term stressor. A three-year capital campaign and subsequent development might be a long-term stressor. In spite of the destructive possibilities of long-term stress, it is important to state that many individuals do quite well under stress and even find some benefit and personal insight in the experience. Leaders of camps and retreats are likely to face a seemingly endless series of temporary stressors in their job. In addition to this, they will have nonwork-related stressors, some possibly long term. For example, a camp director may have to find a replacement for his secretary, deal with an angry parent, and cope with a tumultuous divorce. A series of small stressors may be more damaging to health than a single long-term one.

Another way to divide stress is good stress in comparison to bad stress. Good stress occurs when we are challenged by a problem or obstacle that, while beyond our current ability, is still solvable. In these situations, the body releases adrenaline and noradrenaline, which increase perception, motivation, and even physical strength. Positive stress occurs when we have the following emotions and conditions.

- A desire to solve the particular problem
- The ability to resolve a problem
- Some control over the situation
- Sufficient rest between challenges
- A perceived solution to the problem

Events resulting in bad stress are not perceived as a challenge but rather as threatening or harmful. In these situations the body releases a stress hormone called cortisol, which affects the functioning of the brain in negative ways. Cortisol has been shown to damage the neurons of the brain that are partly responsible for memory and learning. Negative stress makes you feel anxious, depressed, angry, or overwhelmed. In addition, such strong emotions reduce the brain's ability to solve problems and to think creatively. Individuals experiencing negative stress may live in a primitive fight or flight mode in which the only perceived resolution to the stressor is to get rid of it or run away from it. This primitive mode is far from ideal, particularly for leaders who must make important decisions while under stress.

Individuals respond differently to stress. Some people are naturally more resilient than others, allowing major stressors to have no major lasting impact. Others may experience effects that last a lifetime, acquiring a condition named Post-Traumatic Stress Disorder. It is important to recognize that some members of your staff will have less ability to manage stress than others. The reverse is true also.

According to the popular press, there are two ways of coping with stress: Get rid of the stressor or learn mechanisms to cope with it. However, there is a more useful way to deal with stress, involving the following four general coping responses.

1. **Problem-focused coping response**—This is the behavioral techniques that directly address the stressor itself.

2. **Social coping response**—This is the use of others for support, information, or advice.

3. **Avoidance coping response**—This is a response that is aimed at putting the stressor out of your mind temporarily, through distraction or the use of alcohol as examples.

4. **Emotional coping response**—This involves controlling your emotions about the stressor, which often includes modifying how you talk to yourself.

All of these responses are beneficial when you learn to apply the correct response to any given stress. For example, a woman responsible for a sick parent may make use of avoidance response by going to the movies once a week. A camp director may turn to another director for advice over a problematic staffing issue. Another person may directly confront a neighbor about the loud music he plays late into the evening. Each particular stressor will require a different set of coping responses.

As a general rule, if a particular stressor can be alleviated quickly, then find a way to rid yourself of it. To cope with other, long-term stressors, the other coping responses will be necessary.

Rest

Until the very recent past, infectious diseases were the major cause of death in America. Today, however, the typical American lifestyle of poor diet, minimal physical activity, and high stress have caused more people to die from diseases and complications stemming from this lifestyle than from actual infectious diseases. There is still, however, one other influence on general health and therefore leadership we have yet to look at: rest. The need for rest is both physically and psychologically essential.

As detailed in the physical activity section, your body adapts to gradual, progressive overload. Exercise is most beneficial when it encourages your body to adapt to the stress of a physical challenge. However, if you continue to overload your capacity without rest and recovery time, you will reach a point known as overtraining or cumulative microtrauma. It is during exercise that muscle breaks down. During recovery, the same muscle is repaired, but now stronger than before. Without sufficient recovery time, the muscle does not have time to repair itself. Muscle will reach a state of fatigue in which a once successful workout is now almost impossible to perform or, even worse, causes injury. As a general rule, you should not exercise the same muscle group two days in a row and not more than three times in a week.

Sleep plays a role in both physical and psychological health. There must be a reason for sleep since we spend approximately one-third of our lives in this state. And from the perspective of species survival, there must have been a very pressing reason for it since, while sleeping, our ancestors would have been very vulnerable. In the very early days of human beings, if a race had evolved that did not require sleep, they would have easily wiped out their sleep-needing competitors. This suggests that the need for sleep is a basic necessity for survival.

All mammals sleep. Birds sleep. Reptiles and amphibians sleep. Fish sleep. Scientists even found that worms and slugs sleep. Since every creature has a need for sleep, or rest that closely resembles sleep, what are the underlying functions of this requirement? Researchers have still not presented one conclusive response to this question. The most generally accepted answer is that sleep performs a restorative function for both physical and cognitive energy. In one well-known experiment by Rechtschaffen, laboratory rats were deprived of ninety-two percent of their sleep. Their fur took on a yellow tinge, and they began to lose weight. By the end of the experiment, they had lost twenty percent of their body weight even though they were actually eating more food—a whopping two and a half times their usual food intake. After twenty-one days, all of the rats had died (the first had died only thirteen days into the research). The autopsy revealed that all of the major organs were in fine condition, and there was no evidence of nutrient deficiencies or infections. The rats had died for no discernible reason.

Fortunately, few humans are ever as extremely sleep deprived as the above rats were. Those that are react like the rats did. They eat more and lose weight. They have a sensation of losing contact with the world as if they are losing their mind. Severely sleep-deprived prisoners have even been known to die for no apparent reason. What many humans do experience is a sleep debt, often called cumulative sleep loss. If you lose one hour of sleep each night for one week, you will have accumulated a sleep debt of seven hours. This debt can come from late bedtimes or early awakenings. It can also come from fragmented sleep, such as waking up in the middle of the night to use the bathroom. Even a modest sleep debt of eight hours in one week can have the following noticeable effects.

- Blurred vision
- Itching or burning eyes
- Mood changes, particularly an increase in depression
- Lack of energy
- A feeling of being overwhelmed
- Delayed reaction time
- Difficulty concentrating
- Losses in logical reasoning ability

The ability to recall material learned the previous day may be negatively affected by cutting nighttime sleep by as little as two hours. Experiments show that people will not improve performance with a new skill until after they have had more than six hours of sleep. This is particularly problematic for camp directors during staff week. Staff are usually excited about camp and about establishing new relationships with peers, so they often get less sleep, causing a sleep debt. During the same time, staff members are expected to learn much material (camp rules, safety measures, etc.). This sets up a conflict. To resolve the conflict, most camp directors require a mandatory eight hours of sleep for all staff during staff week. Directors cannot actually make a staff member sleep, but they can set a curfew and lights out at a reasonable hour, providing the opportunity for eight hours of sleep.

Most humans need between eight and eight and a half hours of sleep for good mental and physical performance, although there will always be individuals who need more and others who need less. Sleep is necessary for normal mental contact with the world. Sleep debt affects performance, and extreme long-term deprivation can result in death.

Another aspect of rest involves the cessation of physical activity. In one study, researchers asked military personnel to perform physical activity for many consecutive days. Two interesting things occurred. The work completed each day began to diminish after about six days. In addition, and perhaps more startling, interviews with the military personnel revealed that they did not perceive that their capacity to work was steadily waning.

In addition, cessation from work accompanied by ritual and celebration is part of many religious faiths. If your camp supports a faith tradition, consider integrating a day of rest into your program. At a minimum, camp directors should be aware that rest in the form of regular, uninterrupted sleep and a period of time, ideally a full day, during which staff cease their required physical and mental activity is important. Such accommodations will most likely increase camp productivity and safety. In the context of a residential camp setting, these ideals may seem ridiculous, but any improvements made in this direction will help your staff achieve peak performance.

Summary of Key Points

1. Physical capacity composes the very base of the high-performance pyramid. There is every reason to believe that your emotional and mental capacities will not be maximized when physical well-being is marginalized. Without at least a minimal baseline of health and physical ability, you will not reach emotional and mental excellence.

2. There is much conflicting and just plain wrong information avail-

able about fitness. Two of the biggest sources are advertising and well-meant advice from other people.

3. A fitness lifestyle includes four major components: diet, exercise, stress management, and rest.

4. You must set your own goals for physical fitness.

5. There is much controversy over the effects of weight loss for individuals who have no presenting health problems. Diets only achieve permanent weight loss for approximately ten percent of individuals who begin them.

6. Many people are genetically programmed to carry a few (or many) more pounds than they would like. Recognizing and accepting this and then planning and implementing a physical activity plan that takes this into account will help develop a sense of satisfaction.

7. The goal of a diet is fat loss, not weight loss.

8. The goal of an exercise plan is improvement in the four areas of physical development: aerobic capacity, flexibility, muscle endurance, and strength.

9. There is growing recognition that lack of physical activity is more harmful than carrying excess weight.

10. One hour per day of moderate exercise is essential for health.

11. Several principles affect the results of exercise:

    • **Individual differences**—Every person has a different genetic blueprint that affects results.

    • **Use and disuse**—When a person stops exercising, the accrued benefits disappear.

    • **Specificity**—Specific results are related to specific training.

    • **Overload**—In order for improvement to occur, more demand must be placed on the body than normal.

    • **Progression**—The body must be continually challenged in order to improve.

    • **Variety**—A change in a normal exercise regimen must occur frequently.

12. The best exercise program is one that focuses on the development of lean muscle tissue with supplementary flexibility and aerobic training.

13. Stress is defined as the physical and psychological effects stemming from demands that exceed your present coping ability.

14. Stress can be divided into several categories.
   - short-term stress as compared to long-term stress
   - positive stress as compared to negative stress
15. There are four methods of coping with stress.
   - **Problem-focused coping responses**—These are techniques that directly address the stressor itself.
   - **Social coping responses**—These involve the use of others for support, information, or advice.
   - **Avoidance coping responses**—These are responses that are aimed at putting the stressor out of the mind temporarily.
   - **Emotional coping responses**—These involve controlling one's emotions about the stressor.
16. The need for rest and recovery is both physically and psychologically essential.

Conclusion

In the 2001 CCI/USA Industry Survey of Christian Camps and Conferences, executive directors of camps identified their four greatest needs. Four hundred and fifty-five people responded to this question. Fifty percent of them marked the need to "improve my physical condition" as their greatest need. Furthermore, as income increased, so did this need. This is perplexing because camps often sit on real estate that encourages active outdoor pursuits. Granted, most executive directors are no longer teaching swimming lessons, but when their office is at or near the camp, or even when frequent visits to camp are part of the routine, their greatest opportunity for physical activity may be right at camp.

From the same survey, sixty-eight percent of executive directors have "meals served at camp" as part of their benefit package (CCI, p. 161). While the defining qualities of camp food have greatly improved over time, the convenience and ready quantity of it can make dietary goals difficult to meet.

Finally, from this survey, "The one greatest professional problem executive directors currently face in their leadership positions is time management/overload stated by eleven percent of respondents" (CCI, p. 159). Similarly, of polled executive directors, increased discretionary time was listed as their second most pressing felt need (forty-eight percent of the respondents [CCI, p. 173]). These details prompt the question, "When do executive directors have time to rest?"

Granted the CCI study is conducted with only CCI-affiliated camp executive directors. This study sample has particular defining qualities. For instance, ninety percent are male. Nonetheless, we have to wonder what would happen in camping leadership if camp leaders made a commitment to implement the main principles of this chapter?

Try this simple exercise. On a piece of paper briefly note the main principles of this chapter. On a scale of one to ten, rate your current success in each area: diet, exercise, stress management, and rest. Now use your imagination for a few moments. What would your leadership look like if each of these numbers were a little higher? What changes would you see, hear, and feel? What changes would other people notice? How would your professional and personal relationships change? Write down the answers to these questions. Finally, what steps could you take tomorrow (or even today) to begin to make your ideas reality? Write these ideas down. Now, put down this book, and begin to improve your physical capacity.

CHAPTER 4

EMOTIONAL CAPACITY

Overview

Most people have a basic understanding of emotions. This basic understanding, however, does not do justice to the true complexity of emotional functioning. Emotions have served innumerable purposes for our ancestors and continue to do so in modern times. A leader's emotional characteristics play a major role in how his or her followers respond. Unfortunately, emotional characteristics set up blind spots that affect successful leadership. In addition, managing negative emotions can be a major challenge. Increased flexibility and the management of emotional functioning will result in a more successful and popular leader.

Emotions and the Successful Supervisor

Before we launch into the realm of emotions, take a few moments to recall the person you consider to be your favorite supervisor. This person is both an excellent supervisor *and* somebody whom you really like. He or she can be from a past job or your current one.

We may have respect for many of our past and present supervisors. Individuals who are successful in getting tasks completed, as one example, are usually highly respected for their organizational skills. However, respect does not necessarily mean that we like that person. An employee will work best with a supervisor that he both respects and has positive feelings for. Supervisors who demonstrate strong emotional maturity—also known as emotional intelligence—are often the best liked even if they are weak in other important areas. Many people can relate incidents of supervisors who lacked organization or long-term vision, but yet they would work just as hard, or harder, for that same supervisor than they would for a more technically skilled but less emotionally mature individual. An employee's immediate supervisor is often the most significant factor in job satisfaction.

Let's look at Brenda, a twenty-three-year-old unit leader for a group of twenty-eight teenage female campers. She has four female staff members who report directly to her. Several weeks into the summer she approaches the camp director with a sense of embarrassment. She explains that two of her immediate staff members have an "attitude" with her and do not listen to directives. The camp director, a seasoned veteran, asks appropriate questions and discovers that Brenda is finding it difficult to maintain a friendly relationship and be the supervisor with the same group of peers. The director finds that Brenda allowed small but obvious errors to occur early on in camp such as missed meals, oversleeping, and inappropriate language. The two problematic staff members really liked Brenda at first but now appear to have little respect for her leadership of the unit.

It is easy to permit emotions to interfere with or advance leadership. Years later, staff members will likely recall a leader's good or bad emotional skills as one of his most striking characteristics. For example, you might remember one leader who really lost his temper and blew up. Another leader might have been a really caring person.

Refer to Workbook 4.1

As I stated in the introduction, leaders do not often receive feedback from their subordinates, especially if it is critical. The higher the position you hold, the less feedback you will receive. And while positive feedback from employees with whom we have established a good working relationship can be helpful, it is often the feedback from "problematic" employees that would be most beneficial. Unfortunately, this feedback often comes when the employee is angry and has nothing to lose by being critical, such as upon finding out that she is being fired. At such moments, criticism is stated in a way that puts everyone on the defensive, making the information unusable. Criticism can also occur during an exit interview upon completion of employment, but even then it is usually withheld due to concerns over future references.

Would your employees find you an emotionally mature individual? All of us have emotional blind spots, but fortunately we can enhance our emotional maturity. This will create a better working relationship with problematic employees and even assist them in developing their own emotional skills.

Refer to Workbook 4.2

The Psychology of Emotion

Let's take a closer look at emotions. The impact of emotions on cognitive processing is just beginning to be understood. Understanding this impact can have significant implications for leadership. Because of this, we will spend significant time bringing you up to date on the most recent research on emotions.

Rosenberg formulated a three-level flow chart of emotional processing (Figure 4.1).

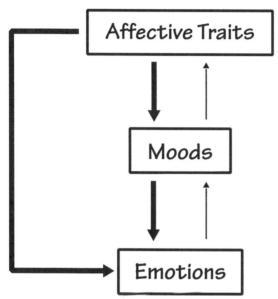

Figure 4.1 Rosenberg's emotional processing chart.
Copyright © 1998 by the Educational Publishing Foundation, Reprinted with permission.
Figure 1, p. 254, from *Review of General Psychology*, 2.

The highest level of emotional processing consists of affective traits. These traits are stable and enduring aspects of our personalities. Some people, for example, are persistently pleasant while others are timid or angry. These inborn traits exert a broad influence on our behavior, thoughts, and motivations.

The concept of moods will be better understood if we first look at the concept of emotions. Emotions are temporary and intense states that directly and immediately affect thinking and bodily functioning. An angry person, for example, will focus his attention on the object of his anger, such as a person or a thing. He will not be able to refocus his attention elsewhere while he experiences anger. Thousands of bodily changes will be going on, such as changes in blood pressure, temperature, breathing, and the chemical properties of the brain and bloodstream. Emotions are comparatively brief but are also comparatively intense. Terms such as *passion, rage, lust,* and *shock* describe both the brief duration and the intensity of emotions. In fact, we can be thankful that emotions are brief, because they create so many physical changes that their continual experience would damage our health. This is true for even positive emotions!

Moods occupy a middle ground between affective traits and emotions. While affective traits create an almost constant emotional background that lacks intensity, and emotions are brief and intense, moods are far less intense but can last for hours or days. When you say you are in "a bad mood," is this different than saying you are "angry"? These two experiences are quite different. A mood may be a pleasant feeling or a gnawing sense of annoyance that lasts for several days. You may recognize that you do not feel normal but also you do not experience the intensity of an emotion.

With this clarification of emotional experiences, let's explore the relationship between affective traits, moods, and emotions, which holds great promise—or threat—for the functioning of a leader. These relationships are shown in Figure 4.1 by the arrows between layers. The placement of the levels does not indicate that one component is more important than another but rather that higher levels influence lower levels to a much greater degree (as indicated by the thick arrows) than lower levels influence higher levels (as indicated by the thin arrows).

One obvious relationship common to all people is the link between emotions and moods. A strong emotion can result in a mood that can last for days. Every reader of this book can relate to experiencing an anger-provoking situation that affected the rest of the week. You may have found that the mood of annoyance persisted for days, long after the immediate intensity of the anger had subsided. However, the effect of emotions on moods, shown by the thin arrow connecting them in the illustration, is not considered very strong. Other relationships are much more powerful. Affective traits have the most profound effect(s) on the other two categories, and it is the only one of the three that can directly affect the other two. The affective traits have the widest and most profound effect on our emotional functioning even though it is the last of the three levels to be available to our conscious minds. It is possible for moods and emotions to influence affective traits, though this is far less common and is outside the focus of this book.

It is important to know your affective traits. Psychological testing can help with this, but it is often too expensive for a camp or retreat leader. The feedback survey in Chapter 8 will offer some insight into your affective traits. You can also begin to understand your affective traits by examining the emotions that you most often experience.

Refer to Workbook 4.3

The Emotional Thermostat

Affective traits can be compared to a thermostat. A thermostat is set for a particular temperature. If the actual room temperature drops below or rises above this set point, the thermostat will turn on a heating or cooling system until the room temperature returns to the set point. Similarly, you will find that you are most comfortable with a specific range of emotions; if you experience emotions that are out of this range, your brain and body will respond by initiating changes to return to the emotional set point. Affective traits, our constant and almost imperceptible emotional background, create the set point. This occurs in two ways.

1. Affective traits limit the moods and emotions you will experience. There are hundreds of moods and emotions that each person could experience in a lifetime. However, each person has a definite subset of emotions that are much more likely to occur. A person whose natural affective state is cheerfulness will experience negative emotions to far less a degree than a person whose inborn emotion is set for hostility. In one experiment, two individuals were asked to maintain an ongoing list of changes in emotions and moods for several typical weeks. How did their lists measure up at the end of the experiment? The pleasant person generated a list of emotions and moods such as "content," "happy," "pleased," and "satisfied." There were negative emotional experiences such as "annoyed" and "discouraged," maybe even "angry," but the quantity of positive emotions far exceeded the number of negative emotions. The reverse was true for the hostile person. His list contained a few sporadic positive emotions but included a great number of negative emotions such as "dejected," "cheated," "impatient," and "angry." People will of course experience emotions and moods that are inconsistent with their set points. We would not expect the cheerful individual to display happiness in the face of personal tragedy. However, on a day-to-day basis, he or she would experience far fewer negative emotions than a person with a hostile set point.

2. Affective traits not only affect the variety of emotions experienced but also their duration. The cheerful person will "bounce back" from a negative emotion or mood much quicker than the hostile person. The hostile person will experience the positive emotions and moods for a much briefer time period than the cheerful person. Emotions and moods inconsistent with set point are experienced for a much shorter duration of time.

Your inborn affective state is how you naturally "feel." If you move too far away from this inborn state, your brain will make sure that you return as quickly as possible to it. In summary, deviation from affective traits, and emotions consistent with affective traits, is limited in frequency and limited in duration.

Let's look at this graphically. Figure 4.2 illustrates the possible range of emotions. The further to the left, the more the emotions are experienced as unpleasant. The further to the right, the more the emotions are experienced as pleasant. The further to the left or right one goes the more intense the emotions become. The following examples demonstrate this concept.

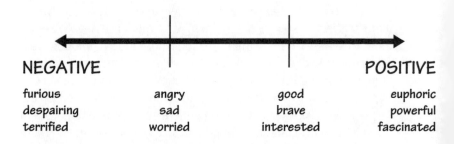

NEGATIVE			POSITIVE
furious	angry	good	euphoric
despairing	sad	brave	powerful
terrified	worried	interested	fascinated

Figure 4.2 Emotional-range arrow.

Karen is a camp director. Her natural affective traits are a mixture of positive and fairly nonintense emotions. Again, this does not mean that she does not experience negative or intense emotions. She will, however, return to her basic affective traits as they dispel, and emotions in this limited set point range will be the most common for her. Some of the emotions that she experiences daily are given in Figure 4.3.

During the summer season, two of her strongest staff members have family emergencies that require them to leave her camp. This immediately

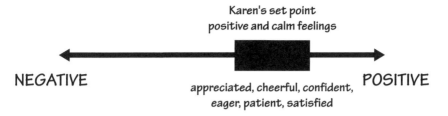

Figure 4.3. Karen's daily emotional range.

Figure 4.4. Karen's emotional slide toward the negative.

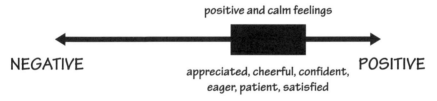

Figure 4.5 Back to normal.

affects her emotions. Remember that emotions are fairly intense but brief. The box in Figure 4.4 has moved to the left to demonstrate the presence of negative emotions.

As the situation is corrected by changing the positions of remaining staff and hiring new employees, Karen's emotions return to the calm and positive range that is much more familiar and comfortable for her (Figure 4.5).

For now, you can begin to identify your affective traits through the emotions that are most common to you. Remember that it is difficult to become self-aware of affective traits because they are constantly present in our lives. Becoming aware of your emotions is much easier and will help you discover your affective traits. Your affective traits will affect your leadership far more than perhaps any other topic in this book. As a leader, if you can recognize the affective traits that constitute your usual emotional functioning in the world, you can then begin to explore the advantages and disadvantages that come with them and be mindful of the blind spots that such traits cause.

Refer to Workbook 4.4

The Emotional Set Point Blind Spot

Similar to the automatic responses of the human body to weight fluctuation, the methods used to ensure a return to an emotional equilibrium are not necessarily in our conscious control or in our best interest. The brain forces a return to its set point, whether we want it to or not. This is true for both positive and negative emotions and moods. This forced return to a set point is one of the greatest challenges facing leaders, because if they fail to recognize its function, they may develop blind spots in their introspective ability (see Chapter 1, pp. 11) and their empathic ability. I will speak more about empathic ability later in this chapter.

Early psychologists recognized the importance of the automatic functioning of the brain. This knowledge, while never completely abandoned, was surpassed by the study of conscious control and thinking. Only in the past several years have psychologists reoriented themselves to the fact that the vast majority of events that occur within a person are completely beyond conscious control. I alluded to this in Chapter 2 when I said that almost all bodily functions, such as breathing and heart rate, occur without our having to actually think about them. Our conscious awareness is, in reality, a very tiny piece of our existence, and it is easily overwhelmed by too much information. The body automatically maintains a balance or homeostasis by placing the majority of bodily functions out of our conscious awareness, though the results in the external world most certainly are not. These can become our set point blind spots.

Nurse Jessica gave an orientation for summer employees regarding the rules and regulations of the health center. Part of the orientation was a discussion about bee stings. Jessica carefully explained the signs of allergic reactions and said that the names of campers with known allergies would be given to their respective group leaders.

Wayne was a unit leader. One of Wayne's campers was stung on a hike. At lunch, Wayne approached Jessica and informed her of the incident. Wayne demonstrated a calm, casual, and easygoing approach to this small event as he did throughout the entire summer. He certainly lost his temper on occasion and was hurt when a camp relationship ended, but, all in all, Wayne reverted to his usual set point of calm, pleasant emotions. Wayne was well liked by other staff and campers during the summer. His interpersonal style seemed to put others at ease.

Jim was another unit leader in the same camp. One of his campers was also stung. Jim grabbed the young boy, placed him over his shoulder, and ran him to the health center. At the same time he left the rest of his group under the charge of a Counselor in Training. Winded and exasperated, Jim described the entire event to Nurse Jessica. He paced the floor waiting for her to perform some critical intervention while emphatically offering his assistance. However, the child was not allergic to bee stings, and there was no evidence that the child was suffering in any way other than from the acute pain at the sting site. Jim became exasperated that Jessica was "doing nothing." Jim was known throughout camp for his risk taking, overreacting, and sometimes acting without thinking a situation through. There was a much more selective engagement by his peers in their involvement with him. He was described as exhausting to be around. Eventually Nurse Jessica had to find a way to get Jim out of the health center. When she asked him where the rest of his group was, he gasped and bolted for the door. Jim was last seen racing through the woods, off trail, trying to find a short cut back to his group.

From Jim's perspective, the world is filled with endless challenges and risks. If it is not, he will create them. Jim thrives on excitement. If asked why he would make such a spectacle of a bee sting, he would likely respond that there was a possibility that the child could have had an unknown allergy. Only a few peers can handle his personality on an ongoing basis. Jim has, without conscious intent, managed to create a world that meets the needs of his set point. Similarly, Wayne also maintains a set point of calmness in most situations, and he has created a world to support his set point. Just like Jim, if Wayne experiences an affective world different from his set point he will act to create an affective world that supports it. Did both Jim and Wayne make a conscious decision to respond the way they did? Jim did not purposely decide to make a major event of the bee sting. His response was automatic based on his emotional set point. Wayne's response was also automatic. The event of the bee sting was a neutral event. Most important, the way they interacted with Nurse Jessica was also dictated by their set point. Wayne maintained a calm working relationship with her, while Jim, ever needing the sense of excitement, had to be beguiled into leaving the health center.

There is little doubt that people behave in ways that elicit responses that support their experience of the world. In addition, these behaviors are often outside conscious awareness. For example, people who have a set point of very intense positive emotions may become risk takers. As children, these individuals were the ones who jumped from roofs. As adults, they jump from airplanes. As leaders, they will seek out cutting-edge organizations that allow risk taking. Those with a calm and positive set point would prefer a more steady and stable organization.

The set point reveals itself clearly during interactions with employees. Leaders who have a set point of hostility, for example, will tend to be harsh with employees. The employees will react to this by disliking the leader. This creates an endless chain in which a leader can ultimately place blame on his or her subordinates for their negative attitude in spite of the fact that the leader was the one responsible for initiating such a destructive relationship. A leader whose set point tends toward sadness or depression will interact with staff in a way that maintains that set point. The same would occur for a leader whose set point was more oriented toward happiness. The following is my favorite example of set point.

George was the owner of a small private camp. He had hired me to help develop better leadership skills, particularly in interpersonal relationships. Most of his staff never returned after one season with him. Staff members whom I contacted for feedback recalled his tendency to scream and described him as easily angered. He was further described as "cold," "rude," and "not accessible." George seemed to be always too busy to have time to form relations with staff. His wife gave a fairly similar description.

George, an intelligent man, recognized that at least the semblance of positive relations with staff would help him get along better. In our work together, George did come across as rude and easily bored. It became apparent that George had a set point of high-intensity negative emotions, particularly intense anger. This range was most comfortable for him but probably not the most productive for a camp director. Then a change occurred. He won a local lottery.

George came into a sizable amount of money. The emotions he experienced were of euphoria, surprise, and satisfaction. These, of course, changed into longer lasting positive moods. Interviews by newspapers created a surge of intense positive emotions each time they occurred. George told me he had never felt so good in his entire life. I believed him. But I also prepared for the worst. George was now way out of set point. He was comfortable with intense negative emotions but was now experiencing intense positive emotions. I knew that a readjustment was bound to occur and soon; homeostasis required a return to the normal range of emotions. Here is how it came about.

The first purchase George made was a new car—a Mercedes. George took it home for his wife to see. She requested that they take the first "official" drive in it together. Now George's wife had quite a temper and was also easily angered. George, who was well aware of his wife's temper, denied her request. He wanted to take the new car over to a friend and show it off. His wife became furious. She proceeded to take a key and make one long scratch on the driver's side from front bumper to rear bumper.

Is there any surprise about George's response? He displayed intense negative emotions. George was furious and hateful. He and his wife did not speak for almost a month. His sessions with me reverted back to reports of strong negative emotions. George, without any conscious intent, had returned to his set point.

Is this incident just a fluke? Was it just an accident or oversight on George's part? George knew quite well that rejecting such an offer from his wife would most likely result in a display of destructive behavior. He had seen his wife's anger head in this direction several times before. Yet he proceeded to deny her request anyway. A single incident can be explained best as an exception to the affective set point, but in George's case it is best explained as the affective set point returning to equilibrium. George's relationships often went through a similar cycle. Hence, summer staff rarely returned for a second year.

We all create a world that brings us the best chance of maintaining our set point. Naturally, events will occur that will throw us off temporarily, but we will return quickly to our comfort zone, except, of course, for major events.

There is no "right" set point for good leadership. That would take us back to the early days of leadership studies in which very specific characteristics were considered necessary for a leader. This is wrong. Each organization requires a specific type of leader suitable for its own style. If a leader joins an organization that does not match his or her set point, such as a reserved and calm leader working for a cutting-edge, high-pressure facility, one of two results is likely to occur. The first is that the leader will fail and be asked to leave or resign. The second is that the leader will begin to ever-so-slowly change the organization to meet his or her own set point needs.

The major dilemma with set point is that in creating a world suitable for yourself, you can lose valuable information. This lost information is referred to as a blind spot, and it is created because leaders fail to see beyond their own affective set point. Successful organizations, from camps to billion dollar industries, require a great variety of input from numerous sources for success. Camps and retreats, however, usually have limited input. Often the leader alone sets the agenda for change.

Refer to Workbook 4.5

The Purposes of Emotions

Emotions are immediate and intense experiences. Like affective traits, they too color our perceptions of the world, though only momentarily. Like affective traits, emotions affect leadership potential.

Evolutionary psychology examines the reasons for the existence of general and specific human characteristics. The underlying foundation of evolutionary psychology is that all human characteristics that last over time serve the purpose of survival of the human species. Characteristics that do not serve this purpose are eliminated through the process of natural selection. Therefore, evolutionary psychology asks questions such as, "What is the purpose of laughter?" or "What is the purpose of tears?" Almost all humans laugh, or cry, or avert their eyes because it served a purpose for our ancestors and continues to serve some purpose today.

Emotions have been present since the beginning of humanity. Even cave drawings reflect the expression of emotions. Similarly, literature throughout the ages gives evidence that emotions played a role in all facets of existence. Therefore, if emotions have existed since the earliest evidence of man and continue until today, how do they contribute to survival of the species? I have identified three major functions.

First, emotions increase self-awareness. Emotions are a signal that something important is happening. For example, two individuals walk through the forest. They encounter a black bear and its two cubs. Person one is well aware of her emotions. She senses danger and stops. Person two has no awareness of emotions. She cannot experience any fear and continues on without hesitation directly into contact with the animal. In this (admittedly ridiculous) scenario, the lack of emotions may well result in a rather unpleasant outcome.

Fortunately, the need for emotions can be demonstrated in much more common situations. A man wants to meet a woman. He goes to a party where there are twenty women in attendance. As he looks around the room, how does he decide which woman he will approach? Without any emotional awareness, each would be of equal interest. With awareness of emotions, perhaps only two of the twenty affect him. Possibly these two cause some type of arousal or cause him to favorably recall a previous relationship. Perhaps they are the only two that are not clearly committed to another partner!

Jack Finney's novel *Invasion of the Body Snatchers* and the film versions of this book depict a world where emotions are nonexistent. Individuals still hold jobs and have families, but they have no desires. The death of a spouse would have the same effect as watching paint dry on a wall. Emotions let people know what fascinates them, what frustrates them, who they love, and who they despise. Without emotions, each day and each person encountered in it would be as insignificant as the next.

Colleen was promoted to director of her retreat facility after the sudden death of the former director. She contacted me because, in spite of her enthusiasm for the new job, she was also experiencing remorse and anger. She had coped with these by pushing them way beneath the surface of her daily functioning, where they stayed silent but ever-present. As we talked, Colleen learned about the value of all her emotions and that the two problem ones for her, remorse and anger, might actually have some beneficial information to offer.

In the brief time we worked together, Colleen was able to better define the emotion of anger. It was really resentment. Colleen had been seriously considering returning to a university to obtain her master's degree when the promotion was foisted upon her. Her quick acceptance, followed by excitement over possible changes she knew would benefit the retreat, forced her to place her true desire for returning to school on hold. Her resentment stemmed from the fact that she had felt obligated to accept the new position as a way of furthering the work of her deceased supervisor. With this information clearly stated, Colleen was then able to decide whether to keep the new position, return to school, or combine the two in a creative fashion.

Wes was interviewing potential summer staff. He asked me to assist in the process because the last two summers had been difficult due to the weaknesses of the staff. As I watched silently, he interviewed five candidates. Afterwards, we discussed those whom he would consider hiring. I could tell that the most important factor in his decision making was that certain candidates gave him a "good feeling." Wes was well aware of the skills necessary for summer counselors but based his decision on a feeling. The most impressive person on paper, and probably the strongest candidate of the five, was immediately dismissed because Wes didn't think she would fit. When I asked him to define what he meant, Wes could only say that she didn't "feel right" to him.

As these two examples illustrate, emotions are a source of information. In the first example, the information was quite valuable and was used to make a very important life decision. In the second example, we see the problematic use of emotions as a guide for behavior. Wes's emotions told him how he was feeling about candidates but had no true relevance to a candidate's abilities. Just because he felt a certain way did not mean that his emotions reflected reality. Emotions are a source of personal information. In combination with thought, they can result in highly informed decision making.

The second major function of emotions is that they prepare a person for action. This second purpose of emotions directly follows the first, increasing self-awareness. Emotions, because they are intense experiences, focus your attention. A camp counselor who is expecting a promotion finds that he has been passed over for another person. The probable emotion would be envy. This emotion would galvanize him to quit, to try harder to demonstrate his competence, or to interfere with the progress of the newly promoted person. Most negative emotions signal that some type of event needs to be corrected.

A counselor on a camping trip with twenty children hears something *large* moving beyond the periphery of the campfire at night. The probable emotion would either be fear or anxiety. Is it a bear? Is it an intruder? Is the thing that lives in the forest from the camp director's story *really true*? The counselor would probably begin making a mental list of emergency or escape plans. Emotions cry out that something needs further exploration. Emotions prepare a person for action.

The third major function of emotions is that they give information to others. Emotions not only signal to the person experiencing them that there is something important occurring, but they also signal to other people the same information. If we see that our boss is very angry, we know that this is not the time to ask for a raise. If, on the other hand, our boss is exceedingly happy, that particular day is probably not the best time to complain about the agency's failings and your general discontent with the job. Emotions in another person also alert us to how a person is responding to us. If we go to a supervisor with an idea that excites us, but the supervisor responds with little positive emotion, it is possible that he or she does not support our idea wholeheartedly.

It is this third function of emotions, the source of information about how another is feeling, that is particularly relevant for camps or agencies that hire short-term employees. In an ongoing relationship, we become aware of another person's likes and dislikes over an extended period. We can learn to interact in a positive fashion. We have the same hope for our relationships with seasonal employees. However, when we are faced with an onslaught of new people, such as at the beginning of a new camp season, it is impossible to know the same quantity and quality of information that occurs in a longer relationship. Therefore, when we encounter emotional responses in seasonal employees, we receive valuable information without actually having any background to help us interpret that emotional response. How a person responds emotionally to a situation can direct us how to respond in future situations.

As part of staff orientation, Dejaun showed a video on recognizing signs of child abuse. Less than ten minutes into the presentation, a new woman counselor quietly, but obviously shaken, leaves the room. Dejaun meets her later and respectfully asks about her response. As he had predicted, the woman had been a victim of abuse herself.

There is no way that Dejaun could have obtained such personal information on all new staff members. This incident gives him valuable insight into how to interact with his employee in the future. Since this staff member left the orientation session, it is safe to assume that most people present would be sensitive to the fact that she might have particular issues with the topic of abuse. Judging each other's emotions will be the primary source of personal information in most seasonal camp settings until relationships have formed.

The implications for this information are huge. Most camp training covers staff competencies related to tasks and camp processes. Any preparation for staff to observe and respond appropriately to emotional responses is usually in the context of staff-to-camper relationships. Staff is minimally prepared to step into perhaps the most intense interpersonal (and intrapersonal) experience they may ever have with a peer group. Emotional responses that accompany the relative isolation of a camp community, the excitement of the challenge, and the fatigue of the schedule occur outside of an established context for interpretation. In addition, the intensity of these emotional experiences may exceed the coping skills of the staff.

A few camps attempt to address this by providing half a day of icebreakers or a team challenge experience as part of their staff training. But few camps provide the time or the tools needed to capitalize on the information available through emotional responses. Camps that take significant time training their staff in how to handle peer emotional responses will benefit tremendously. They will see their staff cope more effectively with the intense peer emotional responses that can come with the summer camp employment experience.

The Emotions Blind Spot

Emotions of staff can be a valuable source of feedback about a leader's performance but are mostly unknowable to the leader. This is another blind spot for leaders. The leader reading this book is most likely attempting to improve his or her performance. The most critical ingredient for performance improvement is timely feedback. This applies to all areas of life such as job skills improvement, sports training, and even learning to drive a car. The observant leader always has available ample feedback. However, in the improvement process, it is the quality of the feedback that counts. There are several reasons that it is difficult to obtain quality feedback. The first is that a leader will, without any conscious intent, mold interactions with staff to maintain his emotional set point. A logical argument here is that since every person has a set point, the staff member would also mold interactions with the leader to maintain her own set point. This is true. Both will affect one another. However, the effect on each other is not equal. The leader has more power in a relationship and, as such, will have a greater effect on the employee. The greater effect is indicated by the thickness of the arrows in Figure 4.6.

Figure 4.6. Relative effects: leader and employee.

The second obstacle for feedback is that leaders rarely know how their employees are really feeling. Employees are highly sensitive to the emotional state of their supervisors. In the past, approaching a tribal leader on a bad day could have resulted in death. It is built into the human brain to be aware of how one's leader is feeling. Your staff members know whether you are having a good or bad day, no matter how you try to disguise your emotions. In addition, if you do try to disguise your emotions, they will know it. This has its own set of consequences.

In the reverse situation, it would not have benefited leaders to be aware of a subordinate's emotions on a day-to-day basis. While contemporary literature and leader training has done much to compensate for this inherent human trait, it has not been, and perhaps cannot be, eliminated. Leaders continue to be far less proficient at recognizing the emotions of their staff than the reverse. This is further complicated because most staff members will not exhibit their true emotions to a supervisor, particularly if they are negative.

Mitch leads the boys' half of a summer camp. All of his camp members have just returned from an overnight camping trip. Everybody is tired and dirty. As the individual units separate to return to their bunks, Mitch reminds the unit leaders that the boys need to be prepared for the beginning of the camp olympics that afternoon. None of the unit leaders say anything. Mitch showers and prepares for the day's activities. Little does he know that his staff members are complaining about his insensitivity to their needs. For Mitch, the silence of his unit leaders indicates agreement.

Some leaders would fall into an opposite category by being hypersensitive to the emotions of others. Being too sensitive to the emotions of others can paralyze a leader when that sensitivity is accompanied by placing too much weight in the decision-making process on how staff *might* react emotionally to a decision. While the immediate and likely emotional state of staff members is legitimate information in the decision-making process, it is not wise for a leader to make decisions based on creating a particular emotional response.

Most leaders do not have this particular handicap. Instead, they are minimally informed of staff members' true emotions. This also does not take into account the very assertive employee. This person will clearly tell you how he or she is feeling about you or about a particular situation. Most employees are not this assertive though. The feedback tool at the end of the book will help you remedy emotional blind spots.

As stated at the beginning of this chapter, staff has developed an opinion of you that is largely based on your emotional skills. The more competent you are with such skills, the more likely you are to form strong, supportive, and even enjoyable relationships with your staff. The best source of information regarding a leader's emotional capabilities comes from the staff. They are biologically wired to be experts at recognizing the emotional aptitude or lack of aptitude in the person who leads them. Here we have a circular problem. To develop emotional maturity, the fledgling leader needs good feedback. One of the sources of feedback is the emotional display of subordinates. But observation and interpretation of these emotions is an emotional skill itself. Herein lies the value of leader training and professional coaching that this book offers. Just by being aware that blind spots exist, you are better prepared to spot your own blind spots. You will increase your introspective capacity. You will diminish your blind spots. You will be able to gather information. You will develop your emotional skills.

Like it or not, leadership has some inherent blind spots because of our biological wiring, our psychological wiring, our emotional intelligence, and the nature of the relationships we have with those we lead. The only one of these that cannot be directly addressed is our biological wiring. The leaders who understand their own emotional set point, develop skills of emotional observation and appropriate response, and strive to understand their employees can minimize their emotional blind spots.

Refer to Workbook 4.6

Anger: A Constant Occurrence

Of all the negative emotions that can occur in the workplace, anger is by far the most frequent. It is guaranteed that in a one-month time period, a person will experience anger. For leaders, a more realistic time period is one week. Because of its frequency, it tends to be the most problematic.

Anger is one of the most researched and yet least understood emotions. Experts have suggested various methods of managing this emotion. For several years, experts recommended that anger be expressed and that its containment would result in health problems. This was followed by research showing that the expression of anger caused health problems. With conflicting information such as this, it is no wonder that most people have no idea what to do with anger. Fortunately, there is now a much better understanding of anger. And yes, there are really ways to use the emotion to foster leadership. For anger brings with it not only the possibility of negative consequences but also, if utilized correctly, the possibility for personal development.

It is important that we look specifically at anger, but before we do, let's examine some other emotions and see what specific purposes they serve. Remember that all emotions inform the person experiencing them to pay attention because something important is happening. Emotions prepare a person to cope with whatever caused the emotion (Table 4.1). They also let other people know what you are experiencing so that they can approach you in an appropriate manner.

EMOTION	PURPOSE
fear	to avoid a threat to self
lust	to increase likelihood of sexual contact
jealousy	to protect a mate from rivals
disgust	to avoid microbes/parasites

Table 4.1 Common emotions.

The purposes of the above emotions may seem quite primitive, and indeed they are. If our ancestors did not experience fear, the bear or the saber-toothed tiger would have killed them. Emotions were necessary for their survival.

While society has made vast changes and advancements, our brain is basically the same model that was used a thousand years ago. Our emotions serve at least the same purpose they did for our ancestors. We experience them, however, for very different reasons. Take fear, for example. We don't fear a sudden appearance of a saber-toothed tiger, though we may justly take precautions against a terrorist attack.

Positive emotions also serve purposes that were useful to our ancestors (Table 4.2).

EMOTION	PURPOSE
interest	to satisfy curiosity
satisfaction	to indicate success or accomplishment
love	to increase bonding between two individuals

Table 4.2 Positive emotions.

Would you be reading this book if you could not experience interest? Would you even care if your leadership skills needed improvement? If you completed a task but received no satisfaction, how likely would you be to do it again? Both positive and negative emotions were major reasons for the shaping of humanity.

Therefore, anger must also serve a purpose. Most emotions are primary emotions. They immediately result from some contact with a specific trigger. We'll use fear as an example. A camp director walks through the woods in the morning to be certain that trail markings are visible. He encounters a black bear. He experiences fear and carefully walks away so as not to disturb the bear (Figure 4.7). This seems pretty straightforward and self-explanatory.

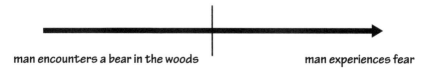

Figure 4.7. On meeting a bear in the woods.

However, this simplified diagram really is too simple. It leaves out a very important step. What if the camp director had never seen or heard of a bear before (just pretend that this could really happen)? If he encounters this large, black, hairy creature with no prior experience of such an animal, it would not necessarily result in fear (Figure 4.8). Maybe his emotion would be interest. How exactly does the brain decide when to initiate a specific emotion? The brain must first interpret what the trigger is before it can determine how to respond emotionally. The brain does this in milliseconds, and we are not even aware that it is occurring. Take the camp director again. If he interprets that the large hairy animal is actually a lost puppy, it is doubtful that he would respond with fear (and it is equally doubtful that he would make a good camp director or live long enough to exhibit his abilities).

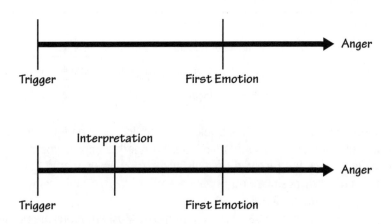

Figure 4.8. Possible result of misinterpretation.

Anger, however, differs from other emotions because it is considered a secondary emotion. A trigger occurs followed by a split second interpretation. A primary emotion occurs. Finally, anger occurs. Anger follows directly on the heels of a first, immediate emotion. Figure 4.9 shows this.

Example

Paula is a director for a small camp. The summer season has been far more challenging for her and her staff than she originally planned. While walking through the camp she overhears two of the cooks discussing her performance. One describes her as incompetent and the other one agrees.

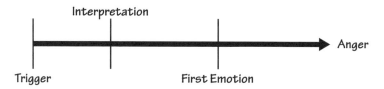

Figure 4.9. Succession of emotions.

What do you think is the first emotion Paula feels?

Most likely, the first emotion was one of hurt or sadness. This was immediately followed by anger. Anger usually follows an emotion that is painful for an individual. Such emotions as hurt, betrayal, guilt, and shame are commonly followed by anger. These painful emotions, when experienced, make a person feel powerless. Anger, however, is an emotion of power. An angry person is a person who feels strong and who is ready to fight against whatever trigger initiated the anger. Anger removes you from a place of weakness and vulnerability and places you back into a position of strength. People do not like to feel as if they have no power over their lives; anger remedies this situation. What is truly amazing about the entire anger process is that our brain does all of this in less than a few seconds.

Although anger serves a very beneficial purpose (especially in righting wrongs), it does have one major complication: Anger interferes with thinking and judgment. When our ancestors experienced anger, the likely result was some type of physical reaction. We no longer live in times when every episode of anger can result in a fight, but our brain is still functioning as if we were. All major systems of the body prepare for a battle or retreat: fight or flight. The brain itself locks its focus on the instigating trigger, and thinking about other things is almost impossible. This hyperarousal of the body and the restricted thinking ability can cause problems for all individuals involved. Anger is similar to all emotions in that it limits the brain's cognitive abilities to a particular focus, or trigger event. Anger may result in a reactive decision that, though it placates the immediate arousal, is a bad decision.

While physical battles might have been a successful resolution for conflict in the distant past, modern life with its complexities and innumerable triggers for anger requires different approaches for coping with anger. The last section of this chapter will focus specifically on management of emotions. Leaders, though, need to be careful with their anger because it can have unintended effects on an entire organization.

The first major reason for particular concern about anger is that it generally stems from interactions with other people. Leaders must deal with a large number of people on a consistent basis while, at the same time, attempting to steer an organization through frequently turbulent times. Employees. Customers. Suppliers. Boards of Directors. The many contacts a leader makes leave him open to experiencing numerous anger-provoking interactions.

The second reason to control anger is referred to in the field of psychology as leakage. When a person is angry, his body is ready for a fight or flight. All bodily systems are on alert. For a person to control this high state of arousal takes a lot of energy and concentration. Yet humans do not have unlimited conscious ability; in reality our control and thinking abilities are quite limited (this will be explored in the chapter on mental capacities). If you are putting effort into controlling your anger, this takes up most of the ability of your consciousness. You cannot, unfortunately, control or contain all signs of anger. You might control your voice. You might control what you say. You might even control your posture. But somehow through subtle body language your anger will be evident. This is why it is called leakage: Some signs of anger will leak out.

Employees, because they are wired to pay attention to the emotions and moods of their supervisors, will spot this anger. No matter how much effort the leader puts into containment, the subtle signs will alert staff. Leakage prevents us from effectively hiding our emotions. Complicating this is the fact that when a leader does try to hide feelings, staff members will see the attempt at concealment and may misinterpret the leader's attempt to hide the emotions. This quiet awareness of a leader's anger can result in an angry camp. Strong emotions are contagious. If several people are placed in a room together, the one experiencing the strongest emotion or mood will infect the others with the same emotion or mood. Similarly, as a leader, you have a strong influence on employees; your anger can provoke anger in your staff. Angry staff members do not make a happy camp or retreat. In many cases, a leader's emotions have more of an influence on an organization than any policy he or she could implement.

Refer to Workbook 4.7

Developing Emotional Flexibility

Certain individuals reading this book are probably experiencing an emotion of contentment because their set point tends to be upbeat and positive.

Others may feel discouraged because their set point tends toward anger or depression. Their set point *is* the reason for contentment or discouragement in either case. Emotions in themselves are neither good nor bad; they are merely sources of information for us and others as well as a means of preparing both the body and the mind for action.

Our limited range of emotions tends to be more problematic. If you are an upbeat person, you may need to exhibit more anger in order to settle serious problems. You may also make poor decisions based on very biased forecasting that accompanies your normal range of emotions. If you are an angry person, you may be very good at expressing yourself, and staff knows where they stand with you. You also probably intimidate staff members who will therefore attempt to hide mistakes rather than face your wrath. Moving beyond the range of comfortable emotions allows a wider variety of responses to leadership challenges.

There are five predominate ways to regulate emotion. Some of the methods are proactive attempts to regulate an emotion before it even occurs, while others are targeted for coping with an existing emotion.

Situation selection This refers to approaching or avoiding certain people, places, or objects in order to regulate emotion. A shy person will purposely avoid social situations. A sensation seeker will ride the most dangerous rides at an amusement park. This method of regulation is quite simple to use and is particularly successful in preventing negative emotions. If, for example, you want to decrease your anger, you could avoid anger-provoking cues. If you want to feel less depressed, you could participate in more positive interactions.

The waterfront director is new this season at camp. Though he is thoroughly trained and knows camp policy, every time the camp director visits the waterfront, the waterfront director is involved in a dialogue with women counselors instead of paying strict attention to the campers in the water.

Camp director one has a set point of anger. He watches the waterfront director from a distance and becomes furious. He calls the waterfront director into his office and gives him seething criticism. This happens during the summer several times. Unfortunately, and purely without conscious motive, he may also retain the waterfront director in his employ because it gives the camp director a constant resource for eliciting anger. Why elicit anger? Because that is the set point the camp director is most comfortable with.

Camp director two desires calm, nonintense emotions. He instructs the assistant director to handle the waterfront director himself and report back if there are problems.

In this example, camp director one seeks out and confronts the problem. Camp director two avoids the situation and unwanted emotions by passing the responsibility to his subordinate. He is also working toward his set point.

Situation modification This second method refers to a purposeful attempt to change the impact of an already existing trigger. An individual finds him- or herself in a situation and attempts to modify it for a particular emotional response.

Carrie is a unit leader. The first night in her new unit, one of her staff members plays the radio the entire night. This keeps Carrie up. Carrie wishes to avoid both resentment at this staff member and irritation due to sleep loss. She approaches the staff member and explains the dilemma. They agree on a plan to prevent a future occurrence.

Attentional deployment This method refers simply to changing one's focus of attention. Attentional deployment can occur through distracting oneself or concentrating on other nonemotional occurrences.

Three staff members must leave earlier than expected during the season. This will leave the camp short of counselors. The director decreases her anxiety through distraction by focusing her attention on the strengths of the remaining staff. If the distraction does not work she may choose to go to a movie in the closest town to take her mind off it, i.e., change her concentration.

Cognitive change This method deals with how one interprets a situation. Recall that a trigger must be interpreted before it can evoke an emotion. How a person interprets an event will affect the resulting emotion. Seeking alternative interpretations gives a person conscious control over emotions.

Chad is informed that the camp director wishes to see him after the evening meal. Chad has almost four hours to wait before that occurs. A requested meeting with the boss is a neutral occurrence—it can either be good or bad. Chad himself is unaware of the purpose of the meeting. On one hand, Chad can begin to recall all of the things he did wrong over the past few weeks; he is obviously being summoned for a reprimand. On the other hand, Chad can begin to recall all the positive things he did over the past few weeks, particularly his excellence in hosting the talent show; he is obviously being summoned for a special thank you and maybe a raise.

Response modulation This final method refers specifically to attempts to deal with an already present emotion. In most cases, these emotions will be negative ones. Anger, anxiety, and sadness are the three most common emotions that people attempt to modulate. It is quite rare for a person to consciously attempt to get him- or herself out of a positive emotion. For example, no one would say, "I'm feeling so good today. What can I do to make myself feel awful?" There are three known ways to quickly change negative emotions; unfortunately their side effects can be problems in themselves: using drugs, having sex, and eating. All three of these can quickly change the way a person feels. Leaders would benefit from recognizing that their staff will also use these same methods to change their emotions. The first two are particularly problematic for camps and retreats because in most facilities smoking and alcohol are banned completely or significantly restricted. In spite of that, drugs could still be used by young people to adjust emotions. Due to the environment of residential camps, sexual relationships among staff members may also occur even though it is forbidden.

Exercise may also be a way to make adjustments in emotions. Camp staff, in general, will be very active. However, this is different than engaging in an exercise routine. If possible, the camp director may want to create opportunities for regular exercise. Such an outlet, particularly for staff members who engage in exercise as part of their real life, may prove beneficial.

A less immediately gratifying but also far less problematic approach to coping with strong negative emotions is through their expression.

Refer to Workbook 4.8

Expressing Emotions

How a leader expresses his or her emotions—particularly the negative ones, such as anger—will leave a lasting impression on others. The previous section explained several ways to regulate emotions other than through direct expression. As a leader, you could avoid situations that elicit the particular emotion. You could attempt to distract yourself. You could attempt to concentrate on something else. You could pass on a specific responsibility to a subordinate or create a regulation banning specific behaviors. You could attempt to formulate different interpretations for others' behaviors. All of these can and do affect emotions. But they are most successful when you are aware that a particular emotion is problematic for you and when you take proactive steps to prevent it. What happens, though, when the emotion is already present, particularly if it is one of the problematic emotions described earlier: anger, anxiety, or sadness? Regulating an already present emotion is always far more difficult than proactive attempts to affect its initial appearance.

When you experience a strong, undesired emotion, there are two possible methods of coping with it: expression or suppression. Expression refers to making the emotion known. Suppression refers to keeping the emotion a

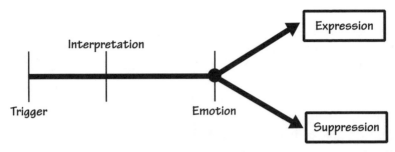

Figure 4.10. Coping mechanisms.

personal matter and not expressing it. Neither of these is always the correct choice; each situation calls for a particular response. See Figure 4.10.

Let's look at the depth and complexity of these concepts. The expression or suppression of emotion is based on two decisions. After you experience an emotion, you must decide whether expression is personally acceptable *and* if the environment makes it acceptable for expression (Figure 4.11).

Denise is angry because one of her employees made a lengthy telephone call when she was supposed to be leading an activity. Denise believes that informing others of her emotions is a way to foster strong and authentic relationships. Denise calls the counselor to her office to express her anger. Denise, by appropriately expressing her anger, sets an example for interaction that is helpful. She discovers that the staff person who made the call had gotten a message that her father had been in a car accident.

Ted is angry because one of his employees made a lengthy telephone call when she was supposed to be leading an activity. Ted believes that an image of rationality and self-control is of paramount importance in a leadership role. He decides to reprimand the counselor in a cool and nonemotional tone. Ted, by appropriately expressing his anger sets an example for interaction that is helpful. He discovers that the staff person who made the call had gotten a message that her father had been in a car accident.

In each case the director responded according to his or her own set point. In both cases the outcome was the same. In addition, the staff member was able to talk about situations and emotions that affect camp operation. Finally, both directors were able to identify that their camps did not have protocol to handle important information.

What allowed this process to occur? Both directors handled their own emotional responses appropriately even though their responses were very different.

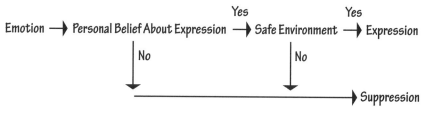

Figure 4.11 Making decisions.

The beliefs that you hold about emotional expression and self-image affect whether you suppress or express particular emotions. Emotional researchers have identified several set point traits relevant to this. Expression of emotions typically occurs for individuals who emphasize drama and passion in life and those who desire intimacy. Suppression occurs for those who are timid or cautious and those who desire a self-image of a rational and antiemotional decision maker. There are those who express only positive emotions but suppress negative emotions. These individuals typically value gaining social approval and making a good impression. Individuals who express dominant emotions but suppress vulnerable emotions value power and aim to be in charge of social situations. This brief list does not summarize all the possible suppression or expression subtypes, but only those that have thus far been identified.

The reason for even including a chapter on emotional capacities in this book is to enable you to become more flexible in emotional use. A general preference for suppression or expression is completely acceptable. However, your role as a leader will require numerous situations in which a nonpreferential style is necessary. In essence, good leadership *requires* a broader range of comfortable emotional expressions. This leads to the next step on the way to expression of an emotion: safe environment.

Simply because you are comfortable expressing emotions does not automatically mean you should do so. The social situation you are in also affects the decision. There is a vast difference between angrily informing an employee that he is incompetent and angrily telling your boss the same thing. Before expressing emotions, you must ask yourself, "Is this situation safe?" and "Will there be consequences?"

The potential for leaders to have problems when it comes to the expression of emotions is magnified because they have power over the people whom they supervise. With the knowledge that there are few repercussions for expression of anger to a subordinate, leaders are set up to abuse this privilege. When you recall the worst supervisor you ever worked for, was part of the reason due to his or her lack of regard for effect of expression of emotions on employees? Male leaders are more likely to do this; females tend to place higher regard on relationships. A leader who believes that anger expression is acceptable and knows that there are few consequences for his expression of such anger can quickly become a tyrant. Unfortunately this may also be a common problem with middle-management positions in camps such as unit leaders.

In summary, the decision to express an emotion is based on two decisions. The first is whether you believe it is appropriate for yourself. The second is whether the environment is safe to express such emotions.

Refer to Workbook 4.9

If you decide, based on comfort with expression and the social circumstances, to go ahead and express emotions, you are really attempting to accomplish two objectives:

- self-expression—to let other people know how you are feeling
- behavior change—to inform other people that they should change their behavior

A camp director who expresses anger at the camp clerk for not completing a report on time is expressing his emotion, which not only alerts the clerk to the perceived seriousness of the oversight but also clearly indicates that the work needs to get done immediately.

There are some ways to express emotions that are more successful than others. A good starting rule is to avoid expression of particularly intense emotion, such as rage as compared to anger. Extremely intense emotions override the ability to think logically. What the leader means to say may not be what the recipient hears. In addition, what the leader means to say may not actually be clearly stated. Also, the leader's emotion is contagious. The leader, after expressing his emotion to another person, may feel better, but what about that other person? What effect(s) does the leader's emotional expression have on the recipient? In most circumstances, the leader has more power. This prevents the subordinate from responding with an authentic response. Many employees will not correct their supervisor even if they are absolutely certain (and with definitive proof) that the supervisor is wrong. If the supervisor is angry, the chances of being corrected are even less. Incidentally, there is striking evidence that those individuals who are prone to express their anger in tirades with yelling and hollering, have poorer health outcomes in comparison to those who approach anger more calmly.

The expression of anger works best under the following circumstances.

- Directed at the appropriate target—Recommendations to punch pillows or throw dishes are not usually beneficial. Repeating over and over again to other people the reasons for anger is also not helpful. A counselor who is angry at her supervisor may talk to numerous other employees but never actually confront the one person who is actually the cause of her anger, the supervisor. These repeated descriptions not only tend to increase the anger of the employee but also inflame other staff members. To resolve anger, the source of it must be confronted.

- Does not lead to retaliation—Most people defend themselves if they are the victims of an angry tirade. This is true of both supervisors and subordinates. However, because of the power difference, subordinates may retaliate through less obvious means such as eliciting the support of other employees or doing less work.

- Results in behavior changes or new understanding of the apparent problem—If the person who provokes the anger in the leader changes the critical behavior or can offer a clarification for the offending behavior, anger resolution is probable. If the camp director is angry because he overheard two counselors mocking him, and then finds that they were preparing a skit for a talent show that mocked most administrative staff, the director would likely be much less affected.

Confronting the source of the anger is truly the best way to resolve the emotion. Successful expression of anger can occur in five steps. Use of these steps also decreases the chance that any form of retaliation will occur.

1. Describe the emotions to the source of the anger. Telling the person that you are angry is minimally helpful because it does not tell the whole story of your anger. Recall that anger is a secondary emotion and, as such, was probably preceded by an emotion of hurt. Tell the person of both the initial emotion and the anger.

2. Specify the exact behavior(s) that led to the emotions. Vague descriptions of why you are angry and general evaluations of the other person's character are of limited value. The specific reason(s) for the emotions are necessary.

3. Take responsibility for your role in the situation, including explaining how you interpreted the behavior. Recall that any particular occurrence can be interpreted in multiple ways. It is important for the other person to understand your interpretation.

4. Check assumptions regarding whether the person is behaving deliberately. One of the common interpretations of a behavior that results in anger is that it was done deliberately or intentionally. Maybe it was. Maybe it wasn't. Ask.

5. Show commitment to the relationship. By verbalizing a desire to maintain a good relationship, the leader is making it safe for the other person to express his or her own emotions and the acknowledgment of a problem.

Try to identify each of these steps in the following example.

"I was hurt and then got quite angry when you overslept for morning call after we spoke about this just last week. I thought that you did this intentionally to get back at me. Am I right, or did I misinterpret this? I really want to resolve this because I want to have a good working relationship with you."

An approach such as this will certainly make it easier for your subordinate to discuss his or her behavior and formulate solutions in dialogue with you. This is the goal of expression.

Expression is the most beneficial method of emotional management. If the leader, however, based on discomfort with expression or the immediate social circumstances, decides to suppress emotions, there are options. Suppression does take much physical and cognitive energy. People who tend to suppress as a general coping mechanism appear to suffer more health problems than those who appropriately express.

There are circumstances in which suppression of emotions really is the only available option. In these cases, first remember that the intensity of the emotion will quickly subside. A mood may ensue, but this is far more manageable and tolerable than an emotion. It too will eventually pass. The leader can perform some of the regulatory methods described earlier, such as avoidance or distraction. Occasional suppression of strong emotions is not going to damage your health. If this method, however, is characteristic for you as a leader, it may be beneficial to seek assistance in expression. There are simply too many occurrences as a leader that will require an appropriate expression of emotion. Just remember that employees are hypersensitive to your emotional state. What might be annoyance to you may come across as anger or even fury to them.

Refer to Workbook 4.10

Empathy

People do not always use words to express the emotions and moods they are experiencing. They tell us instead through the use of body language, tone of voice, and facial expression. The ability to detect these subtle signs will play a large role in how others perceive a leader. To base interactions on verbal content only will lead to the perception of a leader as insensitive and uncaring.

Daniel Goleman in his book *Working with Emotional Intelligence* tells us that people who demonstrate empathy also demonstrate the following emotions.

- They are attentive to emotional cues and are able to listen well.
- They show sensitivity and understanding of others' perspectives.
- They help out based on understanding other people's needs and feelings.

The United States Department of Labor estimates that of the total time we spend in communication, twenty-two percent is devoted to reading and writing, twenty-three percent to speaking, and fifty-five percent to listening. As Hendrie Weisinger reminds us in *Emotional Intelligence at Work*, hearing is a sense that most people are born with and develop naturally according to a set of instructions contained in the brain. Listening, however, is a skill that has to be learned. This includes listening to more than just words. One of the findings of communication research is that ninety percent or more of a message is nonverbal. Therefore, listening means taking in the message from the entire person, not just the words coming from his or her mouth. At the least, empathy requires being able to read another's emotional state and to respond appropriately. At a higher level, it means understanding the issues or concerns that lie behind another's feelings.

Empathic ability increases with physical maturity. Infants experience distress when they see another child start to cry. At the age of two a child begins to recognize that someone else may feel differently than himself or herself. By late childhood, children can begin to experience empathy for an entire group, such as the poor. This progression is not inevitable though. First, as with many of the abilities discussed in this book, some people are born with more empathic ability than others. In addition, a child's upbringing can affect empathy. Children who do not have a parental attachment or who are isolated may not learn how to feel empathy for another person, because they do not receive any sort of emotional tutoring. Finally, people who have little insight into their own emotions are incapable of appropriate empathy. A person must first know him- or herself before empathic ability is possible.

One of the key components of empathy is active listening. A person who believes that he or she is being heard experiences a sense of empathy coming from the listener. The ultimate indicator of having heard another person is to respond appropriately. To listen actively, observe the following suggestions.

- Paraphrase the speaker. This is restating what the other person said in an abbreviated and concise manner. Repeating back what you heard allows the other person to both correct any misunderstanding in the message and recognize that the message was heard.

- Give occasional verbal acknowledgments of listening. The use of brief statements, such as "I see" or "Okay," is proof to the other person that you are listening.

- Give nonverbal acknowledgments of listening. In addition to words, the use of appropriate body language also indicates attention. This includes making eye contact, leaning in toward the speaker, and nodding your head.

- Attempt to recognize underlying feeling statements. This component of active listening goes beyond merely hearing the words. A response to an apparently angry employee, such as "It sounds as if you're mad," is an indication that you are really attempting to understand. Even if you guess the wrong emotion, the other person will correct this and then tell you the real emotion they are experiencing.

It is important to remember that while you are trying to understand a person's message by watching the person *and* hearing their words, they are doing the same with you. And as mentioned, subordinates are better wired and more vested in reading your emotional state than you are in theirs. This list is only as effective as the leader's sincerity in applying these skills. For instance, if you say, "It sounds as if you're mad," but you are not sincerely interested in your subordinate's expression, the subordinate will read your uncaring body language and accept that over your words. You may be perceived as sarcastic, condescending, and uncaring. In this case, you are worse off than before you opened your mouth.

We have already talked about the inability to hide emotions. With these things in mind, you must decide for yourself whether you are genuinely interested in your subordinates' emotional expression.

Weisinger presented a very helpful approach to classifying communication in the workplace, which can be used to gauge the need for empathy. There are four levels of communication in this approach.

- **The niceties level**—This form of communication consists of the mere exchange of pleasantries, for example, "Good afternoon." There is nothing profound in the communication other than a recognition of the other person's presence.
- **The factual information level**—This is the exchange of factual information. An exchange between a camp director and his assistant about mealtimes is an apt example. This does not mean that the involved individuals act like robots without emotion. An exchange of information can be made in a pleasant or unpleasant fashion. Those involved, though, do not go past the presented facts.
- **The thoughts and ideas level**—In this exchange, the involved individuals are actually presenting information about themselves. They are verbalizing what is occurring inside themselves, though the content remains focused on the cognitive level.
- **The feelings level**—In this level, the person is expressing his or her emotions or moods. It is through the expression of feelings that we can begin to connect to other people.

Moving from one level to the next necessitates a greater interpersonal risk. The more information you share, the greater the chance for rejection. Each level also incorporates the levels beneath it. A person at the thoughts and ideas level may discuss them regarding some presented factual information, while a person at the feelings level may present factual information *and* then his thoughts as well as his feelings regarding it.

This has implications for the camp leader. Explicitly using this information in camp training can help shape the quality of communication throughout the summer.

Empathy cannot occur if two people are functioning on different levels. If a leader responds with niceties or factual information in response to another's feelings, in all likelihood that person will not experience empathy stemming from the leader. The two lower levels of communication, niceties and factual information, do not often require an empathic response. However, the presentation of thoughts and ideas or feelings places the sharing person at risk for some type of rejection. It is in these exchanges that the use of active listening is most necessary. It is possible for you to present factual information and demonstrate an emotion at the same time. If you believe that there is an emotional undercurrent to a subordinate's behavior, it is wise to simply ask.

Joan meets with her assistant Colleen every morning for a daily report on the condition of the girls' side of the residential camp. This particular morning, Colleen speaks quietly, avoids eye contact, and appears in a hurry to end the dialogue. Her verbal report focuses specifically on camp with no intrusion of personal information. The director identifies this as atypical behavior for Colleen.

In this example, though Colleen is presenting factual information, there is definitely something else occurring that is perplexing to the director. This is one situation in which asking if there is anything bothering or distracting Colleen is desirable. At best, this question can begin a healthy dialogue including facts, thoughts, and emotions. At worst, Colleen can deny any problem but become aware that the director was empathic enough to notice and care.

Increasing empathy means increasing more interactions in which thoughts and feelings are involved and in which active listening occurs. Recognition of emotions and appropriate responding are the hallmarks of empathy.

Refer to Workbook 4.11

Summary of Key Points

1. Employees will work best with a leader that they both respect and have positive feelings toward.
2. Leaders who demonstrate emotional maturity are often most liked by employees even if they demonstrate weaknesses in other areas.
3. There are three specific characteristics that make up emotional functioning.
   a. Affective traits—stable and enduring aspects of our temperament
   b. Emotions—temporary and intense states that affect the body and the mind
   c. Moods—less intense emotional states that last from hours to days

4. Affective traits, though the least recognizable in ourselves, have the most profound effects in our lives.

5. Affective traits determine which moods and emotions you will most commonly experience. These traits create a lifelong set point.

6. You will return to your set point through either conscious or unconscious methods.

7. Emotions serve three purposes.

   • To increase self-awareness

   • To prepare you for action

   • To give other people information about what is going on inside you

8. Leaders rarely know how their subordinates are feeling. Subordinates, however, are acutely aware of how the leader is feeling. This lack of awareness on the part of the leader reduces available feedback.

9. Anger is the most problematic emotion for leaders.

10. Anger is actually a secondary emotion that directly follows an emotion of weakness or powerlessness.

11. Anger can "leak" out and affect the entire organization.

12. It is easier to proactively prevent an emotion than to change it once it has already occurred.

13. Emotions can be expressed or suppressed. Each specific situation requires a different approach.

14. A decision to express an emotion is based on a knowledge of consequences and the individual leader's comfort with expression.

15. There are numerous ways to express negative emotions. Some methods will achieve much better results than others.

16. Empathy is the ability to recognize another's emotions, to show sensitivity for that person, and to respond appropriately. A leader who has not developed empathic ability risks alienating his or her staff.

17. Active listening is a major component of empathy.

CHAPTER 5

MENTAL CAPACITY

Overview

Mental capacity is easier to increase than emotional capacity. There are, however, numerous obstacles to achieving excellence in this area. The human brain has evolved strategies to make many cognitive abilities appear effortless, even to the point of distorting reality. There are some cognitive obstacles that all humans share, while other obstacles are more specific to certain individuals. There are numerous interventions for improvement in this area.

Each year the *Harvard Business Review* reprints an article at least fifteen years old that is considered a "classic." In 1988, it reprinted one of the most popular articles ever published by the magazine. One piece of evidence for the popularity of this particular article was its number of reprint orders; at that time approximately three-quarters of a million copies were sold. The particular article "Pygmalion in Management," by J. Sterling Livingston, contained the following information: "The way managers treat their subordinates is subtly influenced by what they expect of them. If managers' expectations are high, productivity is likely to be excellent. If their expectations are low, productivity is likely to be poor. It is as though there was a law that caused subordinates' performance to rise or fall to meet managers' expectations" (pp. 46–47). In a retrospective commentary, Livingston wrote, "Recent research has confirmed that effective leaders have the ability to create high performance expectations that their employees fulfill" (pp. 68–69).

The strategy for galvanizing excellent employee performance is apparently simple: Have high expectations for your employees. Even Livingston, however, had to admit that there were far more leaders who could not galvanize the energy and support of subordinates in comparison to those who could. There are numerous reasons for such a problem. In a macroperspective, people in general have less and less commitment to an employer. Individuals keep a job until something better comes along. If we examine the problem a little closer, we can point out many troublesome organizational issues that cause a lack of commitment, such as disruptive infighting between groups, monetary obstacles, or a vague mission statement. If we look even closer, we come to the issues that each individual brings to work.

As you master the content of this chapter you will be better able to recognize your own obstacles.

Emotional vs. Mental Capacity

In the high-performance pyramid illustrated in the Introduction, emotional capacity is shown to have more effect than mental capacity on performance. This may be contradictory to the beliefs of many readers, and certainly to the education systems throughout most of the Western world with their focus on thoughts over feelings. As described in Chapter 4, thinking certainly has major effects on emotions—for example, it is necessary to interpret a particular trigger before we can respond emotionally. However, the reverse is just as powerful: Emotions have a remarkable effect on thinking.

In addition, emotional capacity takes precedence in the pyramid because it is has a much more immediate effect on other people. It is impossible to know what another person is thinking, but we are quite capable of accurately guessing what another person is feeling. Recall that employees are skilled at recognizing the changing emotional states of a supervisor or leader. A leader's emotional capacity will have a profound influence on a camp or retreat. The placement of mental capacity in the pyramid is not an attempt to minimize its importance. Without sound judgment and mature decision-making skills, a leader can inadvertently lead his or her organization into chaos. And mental capacity does stand above emotional capacity in one striking area: A person can adjust or improve his cognitive skills more easily than he can adjust his emotional skills. This chapter will therefore focus on sharpening mental capacities, particularly those that have a direct influence on quality leadership. First, though, we will examine the three great obstacles to cognitive excellence: selective attention, cognitive limits, and the struggle between speed and accuracy.

Selective Attention

Humans have selective attention. We are aware of only a very limited number of stimuli in the environment. The brain screens out the majority of available information. In reality, of the hundreds of things we could focus attention on, most people are aware of *one at a time.* The accompanying exercise in the workbook is an excellent demonstration of selective attention. There is a dramatic implication for leadership in selective attention. That is, no two people will be aware of the same stimuli even if they are in the exact same environment. Each person will focus on environmental information that reflects their own learning style, their own needs, their own habits, and their own level of emotional, physical, and cognitive arousal. In short, we pay attention to what is important to us at both conscious and unconscious levels. Two people experiencing the same environment at the same time have very different experiences.

Example

Jaleel and Angel are furious. While they were on duty for the evening, another group of campers raided their unit. Not only were their campers awakened, but a garbage can was knocked over, screens were pushed out of doors, and several personal items were stolen. In their description of the incident to the boys' camp director, Jaleel and Angel agree on the major details of the incident, but each recalls details that the other was not aware of. Jaleel recognized two specific boys from an older unit, one of whom punched out a screen door. Angel did not see this, but she did recognize another boy who knocked over the trash can. She also saw a particular counselor hiding in the shadows.

Both Jaleel and Angel were in the same place when the raid occurred. Although they agree on the major details of the raid, both saw particular events not perceived by the other. There were probably other events that occurred directly in front of them that neither perceived. Such discrepancies are quite common.

How does the brain decide which information to pay attention to and which information to screen out? There are three general rules that affect attention to environmental details.

1. **Novelty**—The first and most obvious characteristic of an environmental trigger that will grab an observer's attention is its novelty. In the example above, if one of the raiders arrived dressed in a chicken outfit, both Jaleel and Angel would have noticed it. The more colorful, outlandish, or just plain strange an item or event is, the more likely it will be seen and remembered. Just think of the attention-grabbing headlines on the weekly papers available at checkout stands. As another example, on a day trip to New York City with a

group of campers, every single participant could recall the woman walking up the street with an alligator on a leash.

2. **Information that is important to us**—If you take a walk in a wooded area with a birdwatcher and engage her in a conversation, she will have spotted numerous birds without even trying. The nonbirdwatcher would likely have seen none or only those that flew directly into his face.

3. **Goal-directed information**—The third general rule is that our goals will direct our attention. If a person is driving through a new area looking for a place to spend the night, he will be seeking out a hotel or motel. Such places will therefore be attended to. The numerous restaurants and fast-food places might not even be noticed. If, to reverse the situation, the driver is actually hungry, he will be very aware of places to eat but may not see the available places to spend the night.

Because important decisions are made on select information, interactions with employees and coworkers are likewise affected. Selective attention directly influences leadership abilities, often on an unconscious level.

Refer to Workbook 5.1

Cognitive Limits

Most people have heard that humans only use approximately ten percent of their brain. The truth is that most areas of the brain are utilized for some type of work. A more accurate statement is that we have only begun to explore the complexity of the brain and, in reality, know quite little about it. While space was once considered "the last frontier," many scientists are now applying that same label to the brain.

As mentioned earlier, most of what the brain does is automatic and beyond conscious control. This in itself is quite fortunate. If we did have to consciously manage everything going on within ourselves, such as heart rate and breathing, there would be little time or energy left to do anything else. Automatic functioning of the brain allows the time and energy for creativity, problem solving, and philosophical musings. While humans seem to have tremendous cognitive capacity, the true extent of this capacity is still quite narrow and easily overwhelmed. Attempts to focus attention on more than one task at a time present complications. A person attempting to perform two activities at once does neither as well as when he or she does just one at a time. Switching back and forth between tasks—no matter how rapidly—also takes time. Tasks are completed more slowly than if they were approached individually, and accuracy in completing those tasks diminishes. Emotions can limit cognitive abilities. Dealing with strong emotions uses cognitive resources. Therefore fewer resources will be available to use for other important skills, such as problem solving. A person experiencing stress also appears to have a similar reduction in cognitive abilities.

Leaders live complicated lives. They have to deal with numerous challenges, problems, emotional events, and stressors. Their attention is pulled among numerous events. Leaders experience the same cognitive limitations as everybody else.

Example

Eric is conducting interviews for the approaching summer camp season. He has scheduled six candidates for a unit leader position in two hours. He wants to maintain a tight schedule. Not only must Eric review the job application for each candidate, perform the interview, watch the time, and calculate the desirability of each person for the open position, but he must also attempt to create a positive image of himself and the camp.

Job interviews are a paramount example of the problems of cognitive limitations. In spite of how much people may protest, there is no evidence that people are naturally good at this. There are simply too many variables occurring in the interview for any one person to capably manage. Hiring good people is often much more a matter of luck than skill. Fortunately there are interventions that a leader can utilize to increase successful hiring. There are numerous texts available on this topic and just about every ACA conference has some type of workshop on this topic.

In general, making good leadership decisions is difficult due to cognitive limitations.

Refer to Workbook 5.2

Speed versus Accuracy

The brain has to constantly balance two essential functions: speed and accuracy. A trip leader is called upon to make a judgment of the coming weather during a sea-kayaking trip. Her group is about to make an open-water crossing of several miles. They stop for lunch before the crossing. The leader takes time during this break to survey the weather. The group is anxious for a decision with the hope of moving on. She notices the surface winds have become very still and concludes that the conditions are improving to make the crossing. She fails to notice that the clouds have shifted dramatically over the last couple hours. Halfway across, her group is paddling through choppy seas in windy conditions. In this case, accuracy was compromised for speed. The trip leader failed to take the *time* to collect the information available. Ideally, the trip leader would have begun making observations in preparations for this decision much earlier and gathered more complete, accurate data before continuing. She may have even asked for the advice of others. In this scenario, the accuracy of the decision was compromised for the speed of the decision. This is typical of humans. While both speed and accuracy are important, the cognitive wiring inherent in the human brain will favor speed over accuracy.

One reason for the choice of speed over accuracy is that there is simply too much information to attend to. As the section on selective attention explained, there are hundreds of cues in the immediate environment that a person could attend to. Yet even this was a simplification. The study of vision demonstrates the amazing complexity of the brain in making sense of the visual world. The human brain devotes billions of its neurons and trillions of synapses to vision. The process of interpreting visual stimuli occurs even faster than the fastest supercomputer today. Hoffman explains that the image the eye receives has countless possible interpretations. Yet even a child can make sense of a bombardment of shapes, colors, objects, illumination, and motion. Each and every time we open our eyes or look in another direction, our brain must reinterpret what the eyes perceive. Our brain does this so fast that we are not even aware that it is occurring.

As this cursory description of vision demonstrates, there are neither tens, nor even hundreds of visual stimuli that our brain attends to moment to moment. There are thousands, possibly ten of thousands. All of this occurs without any assistance of the conscious mind or with purposeful intent. In addition, other situations of similar magnitude are occurring with all of our senses as we receive and interpret information about the environment.

Add one more layer of complexity. Our cognitive capacity is applied to more than immediate sensory input. Our attention to the present is often interrupted by memories of the past and conjectures about the future. Both memories and conjectures use mental capacity and both have the ability to create an emotional response. All external or internal experiences use a slice of our cognitive pie when we consciously give it our attention. In the final analysis, most of what our mind and body is doing happens automatically while our cognitive capacity affects only a very small slice of our existence.

The major problem with such quick and often automatic processing of information is that misinterpretations are bound to occur.

A cursory glance at any particular item or situation may result in an interpretation that could be wrong. Remember that there are numerous ways to interpret a stimuli, yet the brain chooses one stimulus and moves on whether it is the wrong or right stimulus to give attention to.

A quick review of the preceding information will summarize the challenges that leaders face in making decisions on a day-to-day basis.

- **Speed**—The brain has evolved to place more importance on speed of information processing than on accuracy of interpretation.

- **Selective attention**—Although the brain is coping with thousands of external and internal stimuli every second, only a small portion of such information actually reaches the conscious mind and is available for decision making.

- **Cognitive limits**—The brain can only manage one task at a time successfully, and it is easily overwhelmed by too much stimulation.

Refer to Workbook 5.3

Decision Making

If it were pressed upon camp leadership to describe their function in one sentence, a very likely response would be, "I make decisions." This is not unlike leadership in any setting, but few professions call upon such a broad knowledge base and diverse set of skills. At any given time, a camp leader will wrestle with decisions as divergent as youth development, nonprofit law, information technology, waste disposal, local government, and national trends. The effective camp leader commands a remarkable database of information and a warehouse of skills to mobilize. Understanding the decision-making process from a psychological perspective will help the camp leader become a more effective decision maker.

In 1954, Paul Meehl published a highly influential and controversial book titled *Clinical versus Statistical Prediction*. The book summarized twenty studies comparing the judgments of professionals, in this case, psychiatrists and psychologists, to purely statistical models. The professionals utilized the clinical method in which information is combined and processed in the brain (the word "clinical" in this discussion has nothing to do with a professional field but is only a particular name for decision making by any individual). With the statistical model, the human judge is removed, and the decision is based on strict relations between appropriate data. As an example of this latter method, life insurance agents obtain data on a person, such as age, health status, and personal habits, and plug them into already existing tables and charts that have been formulated to estimate life expectancy. The same agent would be using a clinical decision-making process if he or she made the same estimate of life expectancy on personal judgment. All the studies in Meehl's book showed that the statistical method was either superior or tied with the clinical method. In no study was a personal judgment superior to the statistical method. In 1966, another study by Jack Sawyer compared the same methods in forty-five different studies. The results were the same. There was not a single study in which clinical decision making was found to be superior to the statistical method.

In the decades that have followed, this result has been proven over and over again. Even experts in their fields have rarely been found to make better decisions than statistical methods. Fields that have been studied include medicine, psychology, law, and insurance. And though there has never been a study comparing the judgments of camp directors to statistical methods, there is ample evidence to suggest the same result would be found.

It is important to state at this point that none of this research claims that humans make bad decisions. Rather, they claim that there are much better ways to make decisions, such as using a statistical method. There are those who do claim, however, that humans are not optimum decision makers. And in light of such challenges as selective attention, cognitive limits, and lack of accuracy in comparison to speed, this is really not that surprising.

Additionally, researchers have identified numerous decision-making shortcuts that humans use. They often allow us to make quick decisions without major obstacles.

Shortcut 1: Memory

The first problem we will discuss is the use of information from memory for decision making. Many decisions require us to consider information we have stored in memory because the necessary information is not directly in front of us. The first problem with this tactic is that we use the stored information that is most easily retrieved. A more vivid memory will be recalled even if it is not the most representative example. One of the most commonly cited examples is airline disasters. Statistic after statistic states that flying is far safer than driving. However, when a person is making a decision to travel, a recent airline tragedy could well sway the decision due to the perceived increased risk of danger.

Example

Juliana has arranged with a local women's organization to give a presentation on pedophilia during staff-orientation week. The community paper had recently reported on the arrest of a pedophile in town. Juliana knows that an incident of pedophilia at her camp would result in damage not only to a child but also to the overall reputation of the camp. Staff week is already crammed with activities and presentations. However, Juliana believes it is in the best interest of the camp community to know the warning signs of pedophilia, so she decides to bump another important training topic to make time for this one.

Nobody can fault Juliana in her attempt to raise staff awareness on the issue of pedophilia, but was this the best use of the available staff training time? It is highly probable that the local incident played a large part in her decision. Pedophilia is a very rare condition. Based on such a low prevalence of such incidents, the likelihood of having a true pedophile at camp is slight. This is an example of the differences in outcomes when we compare clinical decision making and statistical decision making.

Approximately half of the incidents of inappropriate sexual contact with children are performed by adolescents aged eighteen and under. In actuality, a sexual offense against a child at camp is more likely to occur at the hands of a peer or a younger counselor or counselor-in-training. A much better presentation during staff week would have introduced this particular material rather than a focus on the relatively rare condition of pedophilia.

Refer to Workbook 5.4

Shortcut 2: Anchoring and Adjust

A second common shortcut in decision making is referred to as anchoring and adjust.

Information obtained early in the process of gathering information, either through memory or an actual information search, is not only a starting point but actually biases further information seeking. In their book *Rational Choice in an Uncertain World*, Hastie and Dawes list several examples of the ways that already-known information biases decisions.

- Because people know that there is a fifty-fifty chance that heads will win a coin toss, they then tend to assume that in four flips there would be two heads. The actual probability of such an occurrence is three in eight.

- Firms and organizations tend to rely on information from the last project in considering the options for a current project.

Information considered early on has a great influence on decisions. However, as with most of the cognitive strategies discussed in this chapter, we have limited awareness of the extent of this influence.

The important point to make here is that humans tend to latch onto information found early in a decision-making process and then use it as a starting point or anchor for comparing other incoming information. If the early information is accurate or correct, this poses little problem. If it is wrong, however, then complications can occur.

Example

Donald is preparing his group of campers for a two-night camping trip. On the previous trip, a different group of campers had managed to reach their destination after a three-hour hike. Donald uses this estimate to set the departure time for the current group.

While Donald's method of calculation is acceptable, if he stops his decision making at this point, there could be unpredicted problems. This current group contains three obese children, the weather is much hotter now than it was with the previous group, and one of the staff members is a replacement and has not been on such a trip before. These additional factors could mean the difference between reaching the campsite with plenty of time for necessary activities, such as pitching a tent and collecting wood, or arriving with an exhausted group after sunset. Donald's decision-making process is no different than that of most humans. Early information is latched onto, thus stopping and biasing further information seeking.

Novelty also makes it easier to recall a memory. Odd and novel occurrences are more easily retrievable from memory and may well become an unintentional anchoring point for decision making, even if their rare occurrences actually make them quite useless considerations.

Refer to Workbook 5.5

Shortcut 3: Anchoring in the Present

Another example of anchoring is through the use of the present to influence memories of the past. Memories are malleable. They are not stored in one particular place to be rerun like videotape or film. They are actually stored diffusely throughout the brain. When a person recalls a memory, he or she is reconstructing it from different areas of the brain. Memory is therefore a reconstruction and, as such, is often faulty. One interesting study illustrates this point nicely. Conway and Ross randomly selected a group of college students to participate in a study skills program to improve scholastic performance. Another group was assigned to a waiting list to receive the same services. The researchers evaluated numerous characteristics of each participant before and after the intervention. For example, they looked at note-taking skills and amount of time spent in study. At the conclusion of the program, they found that there was no improvement in study skills—the curriculum was not successful. They also found that the students who entered the program considered it successful in spite of the fact that there was no improvement in their grades. These students formulated this opinion by recalling an exaggerated version of how bad their preintervention study skills were. They recalled themselves as being worse off before they had entered the program than they actually had been. The group members had manipulated their own memories. The group that was on the waiting list did not, of course, have improvement in study skills either, but neither did they distort their memories of their performance. They therefore did not recognize any improvement in their performance.

Since our present state is our anchor, we unintentionally manipulate our memories so that they match the present. Humans basically deceive themselves. A quote from Valliant sums this tendency up eloquently: "It is all too common for caterpillars to become butterflies and then to maintain that in their youth they had been little butterflies" (p. 28).

Emotions and moods are our anchor. The mood a person is in or the feeling he is experiencing acts as an immediate anchor and influences the memories he recalls. An individual who is angry will more easily be able to recall memories associated with that particular emotion, even if the memories have nothing to do with the immediate anger-provoking stimuli. An emotion of satisfaction will likewise elicit other pleasant memories while, at the same time, inhibiting negative memories.

Example

Brian has a fight with his wife before leaving for his job as director of a day camp. On the way to work he continually runs through memories of all the unpleasant things that his spouse has done throughout the course of their marriage. By the time he reaches his camp, his anger has dissipated into annoyance. His assistant director is late that morning. Brian effortlessly recalls every incident of lateness of the assistant and, in addition, numerous other traits that really annoy him.

Brian's fight with his spouse will likely cause him to put together a much more comprehensive list of annoyances with his assistant. Note that the anger and annoyance have little to do with the assistant but rather stem from a marital squabble. Brian's anger, though, will elicit recall of numerous anger-provoking situations, many of which will have nothing to do with his marriage.

Refer to Workbook 5.6

Shortcut 4: Similarity

When we are faced with something unfamiliar the brain automatically begins to compare it with things that are familiar. If, for example, we encounter a small, black creature scurrying off into the underbrush of the forest, the brain begins to compare the recognized attributes of its color and size to other living creatures we know exist in this forest. The brain looks for the best match between an unknown entity and one we are familiar with. Unfortunately, this search through the brain may only focus on one or two striking attributes, thus leaving out other information that would affect the final decision. Because two items have similar attributes does not make them similar.

Example

Claire was approached by two counselors today regarding a female camper in their group. The camper will not listen, seems hyper all the time, is constantly talking, and is increasingly uncontrollable. Claire immediately surmises Attention Deficit Hyperactivity Disorder (ADHD). The camper has acknowledged symptoms of the condition, such as restlessness, hyperactivity, and trouble controlling behavior.

Claire may be accurate in her diagnosis of ADHD. The characteristics of the child are indeed similar to symptoms of a child with such a condition. Could it, however, be something else? Just as in the earlier example of offering training for pedophilia in a camp setting, knowledge of the common traits for the condition could influence the final decision. ADHD occurs in three to seven percent of school-aged children. It is therefore unlikely that the characteristics of the child indicate this medical condition. The child may be reacting to the stress of leaving home for the first time. She may be having a mild allergic reaction. She may be constipated, or she may simply be a particularly energetic individual. There are numerous other ways to understand the behaviors.

The real problem with this shortcut in this example is that once a counselor or director has decided that ADHD is the cause of the problematic behaviors, it is likely that staff will begin to treat the child differently. It is then likely that the child will ultimately be sent home by a frustrated staff with a recommendation to seek medical assistance.

Refer to Workbook 5.7

Shortcut 5: Randomness

One of the most interesting of the shortcuts for decision making is the belief that randomness can be managed. Sports players who are having a successful period in their career may attempt to maintain an extremely set routine so as not to affect their winning streak. They may, for example, eat the same food every day and wear the same "lucky" jersey each game. Camp directors, similarly, may attempt to rehire the exact same staff and keep the same schedule after a particularly successful season. Ultimately, we must question whether these efforts actually make a difference.

Random events occur. This is not news to anybody. But people act as if they have more control over their lives than they really do. Langer, for example, found that individuals, in spite of knowing that the total of a dice roll is completely random, threw the dice harder when attempting to obtain higher numbers.

If an event is purely random, such as a tossed coin landing on heads, there are bound to be occasional patterns that appear. A person may toss heads five times in a row. The chances of such an event occurring is statistically low, but it most certainly does happen. It does not mean, though, that the thrower has achieved a power over the coin. This is merely an apparent pattern in randomness. A camp may have two good seasons in a row. It could be due to the excellence of the director and the staff, or it could be just a random pattern. No one can ever know. Making decisions as if a pattern exists when, in reality, the occurrences are purely random can cause difficulties.

Directors need to allow for the fact that, in spite of their best efforts, randomness will occur. This randomness may affect outcomes negatively or positively. A fantastic summer season may be due to an amalgam of factors that will never happen again. It behooves directors to take a long-term perspective and analyze several data sets, such as parental complaints, employee turnover, and employee satisfaction to really see if a camp is heading in the right direction.

Example

Keith began a counselor-in-training program for the first time last summer. He approached the project with a sense of excitement and trepidation. The project was very successful. He therefore uses the same curriculum and guidelines for the following summer. In fact, due to the success of the first season, Keith does not put much energy into planning the program. However, this summer he ends up sending two of the participants home, and he is continually frustrated by the program. He is considering dropping the project completely for future seasons.

Is the counselor-in-training program flawed, or is the weakness of the second season just a random bad event? Is it even possible that the successful first season was merely a fluke? Based on the information we have available, we just can't tell.

This section has introduced the topic of decision making. Humans make less than successful decisions for numerous reasons. Selective attention and cognitive limits affect the process. There are also shortcuts the brain uses to speed the process. Remember that speed takes precedence over accuracy. So while these shortcuts do decrease the amount of time that is utilized for decisions, they *may* also result in a less than optimum decision.

- **Memory**—Human beings make much use of information stored in their memory for decisions. What is remembered, however, may be very biased or selective.

- **Anchoring and adjust**—The first piece of information encountered, either in memory or as a factual piece of external information, may inadvertently become a starting point for decisions, even if the information is wrong.

- **Anchoring in the present**—How a person is thinking and feeling in the present manipulates recall of memory.

- **Similarity**—Decisions are made on the limited comparisons of similar attributes.

- **Randomness**—Decisions are made based on apparent patterns that are actually random events.

Other shortcuts have been found but are too complicated for this book

There appears to be an agreement among researchers that the current decision-making strategies utilized by individuals are not optimal. Such strategies will not necessarily result in the best possible decision, and they certainly do not stack up well to statistical decision making. However, such shortcuts work because we are able to make acceptable—if not the best—decisions in stressful, challenging, or overwhelming situations. This could be restated as an ability to make acceptable decisions in daily life. The decision-making shortcuts enable the decision maker to get through the myriad complications of existence.

There are strategies for formulating better decisions. The conclusion of this chapter will introduce some such strategies.

Cognitive Distortions

The following examples will clarify this information.

- Chuck has been called to meet with the camp director. As he approaches the main office he is thinking, "Uh-oh. I'm about to be fired."

- Wyllis notices his girlfriend yawn while he is talking. He thinks to himself. "She doesn't care what I'm saying."

- Faith receives a phone call in the middle of the night. As she stretches over the bed to answer it she is thinking, "Oh, my God! What happened?!"

Each of these individuals had thoughts appear in their head without any conscious intent. Thoughts, however, can be faulty. Because a thought appears inside our heads does not necessarily mean that it is valid. In the above example involving Wyllis, his interpretation of his girlfriend's yawn is that she doesn't care about his conversation. This could be true. It could also be false. There are numerous other interpretations for the behavior. If Wyllis accepts his immediate interpretation, he may become angry and behave differently toward her.

Thoughts are important because they directly affect how a person feels and behaves. There are patterns of problematic thinking that we can call distorted thinking patterns. This does not refer to situations where one needs professional psychiatric help. For the context of this book, *distorted thinking patterns* refers to the set of mistakes in thinking that a person is most prone to make. Each individual has a particular set of distortions that is typical for him or her. Like the other effects on mental capacity described earlier in this chapter, the reason for the presence of distortions is to speed the thinking process. Cognitive distortions enable a swift interpretation of events so that the person affected can quickly respond. Distortions are a much more compulsive version of thinking than a rational, methodical, and therefore slower approach.

Some common distortions follow.

All or Nothing Thinking

This distortion is also referred to as "black and white thinking." It refers to interpreting events in the extreme positive or the extreme negative. Take our interpretations of other people for example. We probably know some people who are really good people, and we might know some individuals who are pretty bad. It's doubtful, though, that we know anybody who is completely, a hundred percent good or bad. Everybody has good and bad qualities. One common example occurs during the dating ritual. It was, and continues to be, inevitable that some staff members will become romantically involved during the course of summer camp. During the early stages of the relationship, the staff members would report that their boyfriend or girlfriend was perfect or incredible or just a great person. It was difficult for these staff members to see the negative qualities of their chosen partner. Unfortunately, after the first argument, the other extreme emerged. Suddenly the same boyfriend or girlfriend was an unfeeling monster or the worst person in the world. Now each could barely see the positive characteristics of the partner.

If our thoughts are telling us that a person, a thing, or an experience is the absolute worst, and we accept this interpretation without investigation, we are having unpleasant feelings and responses to the trigger. One component of cognitive therapy is slowing down the thought process so that individual thoughts can be recognized. Once again, because a thought pops into our head, it does not immediately mean that it is true. All or nothing thinking is one of the most common distortions experienced and, as such, does play a part in leadership. See if you can spot this thinking distortion in the next example.

Example

Arnold is a director for a small camp. He has had some challenges with staff during the summer and even had to let one person go. He is hoping that the remaining few weeks can speed by without incident. On making his rounds through the camp one afternoon, he comes across a male staff member berating a young camper loudly in a cabin. One policy in camp, and explained during staff week, is that no disciplinary action should occur without at least one other adult present. The following thoughts immediately come into Arnold's head.

> "I don't believe this! Doesn't this #$%^& know not to be yelling at a kid like that? *And* he's alone with him in a cabin! This guy is an absolute idiot! I guess this is another termination."

Arnold certainly has a right to be angry, and there may even be a need for disciplinary action against him. However, immediately labeling the staff member with the extreme title of "absolute idiot" may prevent proper investigation. Is there an explanation for the incident? Could this child have done something so preposterous that even the most mild-mannered person would respond with yelling? Remember that staff members may have the same distortions. They may begin to separate children into the good group and the bad group when, in reality, most children will fall somewhere in between.

Exaggeration of the Positive or Negative

This second distortion is similar to all or nothing thinking. The importance of a pleasant or unpleasant event is greatly exaggerated. One camp director I worked with related an account of his senior prom. He had spent a small fortune on the tuxedo rental, limousine rental, flowers, and prom tickets. On the morning of the prom, he awoke with a small pimple on the side of his nose. From a distance of a foot or more it was completely invisible. This tiny pimple, however, destroyed his prom. He tried to keep the affected side of his face away from his date. He would not let anyone take a picture of him. And, probably the worst for him, he could not keep his concentration off the pimple. He worried about it the entire evening.

The importance of positive events can also be exaggerated. A male and a female teenager on opposite sides of the buffet make eye contact for a moment. The male immediately and involuntarily thinks that this indicates a sexual interest on the part of the female. In actuality the eye contact, from the perspective of the female, could mean interest. It could also be a neutral, social courtesy. It could be that the female was smiling at something completely unrelated and happened to make eye contact. In any event, the male has a thinking distortion in regard to the brief event and acts on his distorted thinking. The potential for a sexual offence is set up.

Part of correcting distorted thinking, in addition to recognition of problematic thoughts, is learning how to think more realistically. A person can reduce anxiety by recognizing how he or she has exaggerated the unpleasantness of a situation and by examining his or her own thinking. As stated earlier, emotion also interferes with decision making. Through calming of the emotion, one can appraise possible solutions more effectively.

Minimization

This distortion is the opposite of exaggeration. With this distortion, the effects of a potentially serious occurrence are underestimated. Many adults and adolescents who are incarcerated knew that their criminal act could get them into trouble. What they failed to consider was the extent of the consequences. Once again, in my clinical experiences with such teenagers, I have heard a common theme. While they did indeed know that the theft (or the assault, or the drug use, etc.) could get them into trouble if caught, they only considered a restricted range of consequences such as suspension, punishment by parents, or some other lesser result. Yes, they did know that what they were doing was illegal, but they did not consider actual, legal consequences as a possibility.

This distortion happens most often when a person really wishes to do something that he or she knows is wrong or inappropriate.

Example

Eddie is a new counselor at camp this summer. He, along with the rest of the staff, was informed of the camp boundaries. No males are to be in the female section of the residential camp after dinner. It is now after midnight. He is dressing himself in all black clothing so as not to get caught as he sneaks over to the girls' side. Eddie doesn't really think he will be caught. If he does, all he faces is a harsh lecture from the director.

In some camps, Eddie may face more than a harsh lecture. Minimizing the possible consequences of an act enables a person to pursue the activity with a sense of confidence. The more a person desires something, the less likely he or she will consider the full range of possible consequences of the act. Eddie might be grievously surprised to find himself charged with sexual assault as the state police take him away rather than the stern lecture he really never expected anyway.

Personalization

This final distortion refers to an immediate thought that an event is personally directed at the individual. Recall that in the discussion of anger from

Chapter 4, one common anger-eliciting interpretation is that an offending act is personally directed at the leader. The tendency to personalize an event can assume either a negative or a positive tone.

Example

Jessie is the waterfront director at a residential camp. While he is in the local town one evening on an off-duty night, several counselors enter his cabin and remove all of his shoes. Jessie does not notice their absence until the next morning. He immediately thinks that he has been robbed and that he was personally targeted because of his strictness at the waterfront. He is sure that this act was due to staff dislike for him. As he hurries to the camp director's cabin to complain, and possibly to threaten to quit if his shoes aren't returned, he notices all of his shoes tied to the top of the flagpole. The camp director later explains that this is an unfortunate tradition at camp and that at some point during the summer, every person with a title of director will find a personal item hanging from the center-camp flagpole.

Jessie immediately thought that he had been targeted. This thought only resulted in anger and a need for retribution. It is quite possible that he was targeted as the first person for the camp prank because he was disliked. It is also possible that he was targeted first simply because he wasn't there that night, thus making the pranksters' task relatively easy.

The first thoughts that occur automatically after an event are often assumed correct. In extreme examples, it would be easy to recognize the ridiculousness of such a method of interpretation. If Jessie had run to the camp director and complained that some black bears under the leadership of a raccoon had skillfully entered his cabin and removed his footwear, all sane people would rightfully doubt the explanation. However, if the first interpretation is plausible, people will react on it as if it is indeed true.

We will look at one more recognized problem with mental capacity before delving into some of the solutions that researchers have developed to manage cognitive distortions. Fortunately, in the case of cognitive distortions, there is an easy solution. Except in life-threatening situations in which rapid thought means the difference between safety and danger, always question the first interpretation of an occurrence. With practice, a person can recognize automatic thoughts and then investigate them for their validity.

Refer to Workbook 5.8

Personal Maps

In order to reduce the demand on our already limited cognitive abilities, the brain has developed so that most of its activities occur automatically and without conscious knowledge. The brain has developed "maps" of what occurs typically in our lives so that they can be followed without the need for judgment or decision making. Use fast food restaurants as an example. Without any conscious consideration on our part, we know what will happen when we enter one of these franchises. We wait in line, place an order, pay the counter person, and either sit down to eat or leave with the food. Throughout the entire process, the person involved may be considering work-related items or merely what particular item to order that day. He is not coaching himself on what step is supposed to occur next when ordering food in such a place. Ordering food at a fast food restaurant can be seen as one route of thinking and actions on one map for those who are familiar with this task.

Imagine what would happen if this same individual, after placing his order, was suddenly handed an apron and instructed to step behind the counter and cook it himself. The person would be dumbfounded. Much of the comedy on hidden-camera television shows comes from breaking obviously held but not consciously recognized expectations of how the world works. A person who throws a bowling ball down the aisle may not be able to predict what pins will tumble, but her expectations are certainly challenged when the ball stops halfway down the aisle and then rolls back again to meet her. A person at an all-you-can-eat salad bar knows the rules of standing in line, taking a plate, and putting food on it. He is quite surprised to be confronted by a surly staff member telling him he took too much and that he needs to put some food back. These comedic set-ups are a direct affront to a person's unstated personal maps of how the world is supposed to be.

Expectations can result in less than amusing dilemmas. Sometimes the results can be horrifying. The unforgettable day of September 11, 2001, is a paramount example. The passengers in the airplanes that struck the World Trade Center and the Pentagon likely had a map in their mind of what a hijacking consists of, such as an expectation that the plane would be taken to another location and be held there until certain demands were met. Until that day, few, if any, people held an expectation that a hijacked plane would be used as a bomb. Furthermore, probably very few people who got on any plane in the United States on that day accessed their personal map related to hijacking. Without even thinking about it, they had ruled out such a possibility for their flight. Now the model in the human mind of what is supposed to happen during a hijacking is forever shattered, and that map is most likely accessed much more frequently.

Expectations are best explained as our understanding of how we think the world is supposed to be. We can go about our lives without having to consider every move we make. It is important to realize, though, that these expectations exist only in our heads. They are not wholly accurate descriptions of the real world. We may use an actual paper map when attempting to travel to an unfamiliar place. The map can give good instructions on how to get from one place to another, but it cannot inform us of route changes since the printing of the map, traffic delays, weather disruptions, or car troubles. Likewise, the maps we have in our head are satisfactory enough to get us by on a day-to-day basis, but they leave us unprepared for unexpected events.

The following specific problems result from our personal maps.

Expectations Guide Perception

One of the first topics introduced in this chapter was selective attention. People must limit their awareness of the innumerable sensory stimuli that bombard them. One method the brain uses for selection is to focus on information that is important to an individual. Expectations help guide how a person will focus attention. People whose map of the world show it to be a dangerous place that is fraught with hazards will focus their attention on news reports that affirm this view, such as murders, assaults, and other tragedies. A person who has a less bleak view of the world will encounter far more stories of charity and positive social involvement.

Example

Camp director Charles has an unacknowledged expectation that camp is supposed to run smoothly. Yes, there will be some challenges over the season, but nothing that can't be dealt with. Brian, his assistant, has a far less comforting expectation of the world. He believes that people are always looking out for themselves and that they require constant supervision to ensure quality work. Charles barely leaves the front office during the season, while Brain goes out to watch the staff in action every day. At the end of the season, director Charles congratulates himself on the hiring of such an excellent staff. Brian, on the other hand, would never hire back any of these lazy and self-centered staff members.

Charles, because he did not leave the office, never truly saw his staff in action. Brian may have a more accurate opinion, but his too is biased. Though he saw the staff in action constantly, we are not sure of his cognitive distortions. It is also probable that he did not see the numerous positive behaviors of the staff. His focus on their negative activities may have literally blocked him from perceiving the good, and even great, things the staff did.

Expectations Can Lead to False Memories

Memory is malleable. A person can reconstruct the past so that it is a more comfortable fit with one's expectations. This is similar to using the present as an anchor for a decision-making shortcut.

Example

Yolanda recognizes that her staff members need more training. She also recognizes that this particular facet of camp leadership is not her strong point. After a difficult season last year, she decides to hire a consultant to complete the staff orientation this summer. Her expectation is that this will result in a far more capable staff. At the conclusion of the summer, she realizes that the summer truly was far better than the previous one. She now knows that hiring an outside consultant is a better way to train staff.

Is Yolanda right? It could be that the consultant made a difference. It could also be that the consultant really achieved nothing except to influence Yolanda's expectations. Yolanda may actually be recalling an exaggerated version of how bad the previous summer had been so as to match the expectation that this summer, with the help of the consultant, was more successful. Other factors also likely played a role—it is hard to separate out all of the cognitive influences. Yolanda could have selectively attended to the more positive occurrences in camp this summer and avoided the negative. Maybe the previous weak year was a random event, and this summer would have been good even without the consultant. She may be using a cognitive distortion to exaggerate the positive benefits of the consulting intervention. There is not enough information to know the answers.

It is simple to demonstrate the effect that expectations can have on our interpretation of events. Most people have a basic familiarity of the placebo effect. This is usually defined as an inactive substance given to a patient under the guise of actual medical treatment. One startling experiment shows the power of the placebo effect. Thirteen students were touched on one arm with leaves from a harmless tree but told that they were the leaves from a poisonous tree. All thirteen displayed skin reactions to the leaves.

More current research has found that expectations can influence pain, anxiety, depression, warts, drug and alcohol use, and sexual arousal. If a person's expectations can affect such a wide variation of responses, it would be foolish to think that leadership is not likewise influenced by the expectations that go along with a leader's personal maps.

Solutions

A leader might have a comprehensive understanding of the effects of societal change and even of organizational dynamics, but without an understanding of himself, this information is useless. The reason why so many leaders unwittingly continue to adversely affect staff is because human behavior is remarkably resistant to change. Each person has developed an emotional set point, a set of cognitive distortions, selective attention, and an internal map of the world. Our brain will fight to maintain our homeostasis even if we know that certain changes would actually be very beneficial.

Fortunately, adjusting our cognitive capacity is easier than a change of emotional capacity. With cognitive capacity, simply taking a course in probability might result in dramatic changes in decision-making approaches. Cognitive therapy teaches individuals how to regulate distorted thinking, often with strikingly successful results. Just slowing cognitive processes increases our accuracy. Remember that the brain prizes speed over accuracy. Self-awareness, the consideration of options through a lens of rationality, and the assessment of probability rather than immediate shortcuts help the leader maximize his or her cognitive capacity.

Solution 1: Make Use of Other People

Since every person has selective attention and a different understanding of how the world is supposed to be (a personal map), each person will necessarily have a different perspective regarding a problem. Another person may have just the information that is needed to make the best decision. Leaders of camps and retreats who make unilateral decisions would likely fail in the big business world where input from various sources is considered essential.

Having sat through many strategic planning meetings with administration, board members, and staff, I am always amazed at how different the perspectives are among the three levels. Each of the levels has information that is not only beneficial, but often invaluable. Without the sharing of the different perspectives, the completed strategic plan would be missing relevant information. Gathering information from other people is probably the most simple of the solutions for increasing cognitive capacity. Beware, though. There appears to be a limit to the amount of information that a person can use to formulate a decision. Once again, the brain can only focus on one particular piece of information at a time. Research shows that too much information can result in as weak decision making as too little information. Confidence in one's decisions may rise with increased information, but even two or three complex variables beyond the optimal amount of information may outstrip human cognitive capacities. Judgmental accuracy is highest when there are between five and nine pieces of information present. Gathering the opinions of five people who may have a perspective on the immediate problem may allow just the right amount of additional input for successful decision making.

Solution 2: Apply Data Sorting

If the leader has sought the opinions of several other people, he or she is now faced with an additional challenge of how to weigh the importance of each piece of information. Although additional information can increase accuracy, humans often fail to adequately select the most salient data and then, even further, to successfully integrate them.

Medicine and psychology have made increasing use of statistical models but continue to utilize sound clinical judgment. These fields, therefore, have invested much energy into research on such judgments. Several guidelines have been formulated as follows.

- Recognize that one's confidence in one's own decision-making and judgment skills has very little to do with the reality of making right and good decisions.
- Do not depend on insight alone.
- If a statistical model exists for a particular problem, use that model.
- Minimize reliance on memory. The use of external aids such as written records, computers, and even handwritten notes permits less reliance on the memory. By not having to purposefully keep particular information in memory, the brain is able to use its capacity to focus on other more pressing information.
- Maintain multiple hypotheses. When multiple hypotheses are considered, the brain is forced to obtain more accurate information from memory. The use of multiple hypotheses also increases the chance that one of them might indeed be right.

Solution 3: Accept Randomness and Uncertainty

Superstitious behavior is an attempt to control randomness and uncertainty. One individual was convinced that touching the top of the door to his house each time he passed it would prevent any harm from coming to his family. On a logical level he knew that this was utterly ridiculous, but he insisted on doing it anyway. Every person demonstrates some type of superstitious behavior, including leaders.

Leaders often believe that any problems that occur under their leadership reflect on their abilities. If a camp director is informed of a damaged bench on the playing field, and does not order a repair, an accident involving the broken bench can be traced back to the director. Many times, though, leaders have little control over what happens. Part of the science of leadership is the acceptance of uncertainty and randomness in the events that occur under one's leadership. Unfortunately, randomness and uncertainty can be frightening.

Humans are left with conflicting desires. Many people wish to reduce the amount of uncertainty in their lives. Yet a life without uncertainty could well be a nightmare. How many people would want to know the exact moment of their death? How many would want to know that they are about to lose somebody they love dearly and yet be powerless to change it? It is only because we do not know what the future holds that we are able to aspire, to dream, to make plans, and to make choices.

The reality of life, and perhaps a joyful reality, is that we truly have limited control over our own lives. It's not that we can blame uncertainty and randomness for all our shortcomings and problems, but we can welcome them as an opportunity to change and grow. Even our own brains and bodies are influenced more by their genetic blueprints than through any conscious control on our part. For a leader to assume that she has more control than she really does is a setup for an eventual disappointment. The one thing we can do is to make the best decisions that affect ourselves, our staff, and our organization. Science has fortunately given us the tools to help formulate such decisions.

Solution 4: Have Variety in Choice Strategies

One way of dividing strategies is to classify them according to the amount of mental effort each one requires. Recall that humans will most often make use of the least time-consuming strategy even if it results in a less than optimal decision. The least time-consuming equates with a minimal amount of required mental effort. The workbook walks you through a detailed example of both inadequate and comprehensive strategies. I strongly recommend that you examine this material.

Solution 5: Use Rational Choice

A good decision is one in which the final choice among the available alternatives results in the achievement of the decision-maker's goals. While this seems like common sense, the unfortunate fact is that people often do not make good decisions even when they have set good goals. Goal setting is itself a decision-making process, and it is beyond the scope of this book. The numerous cognitive obstacles presented in this chapter are impediments to successful rational decision making. However, as Hastie and Dawes recommend, rational decision making can be a valuable tool. Observing the following three guidelines will minimize cognitive obstacles when using a strategy of rational choice.

1. *Decisions are based on current assets.* These assets can be financial, scheduling, psychological, romantic, and even emotional. The assets exist currently and can be affected by the results of the decision. On the contrary, a sunk cost is a past expenditure of time, money, or energy that cannot be recovered or refunded.

   For example, Dorothy is considering adding a climbing wall to her camp. She hesitates because the ropes course she added three years ago was never as successful as she had planned. While the campers did enjoy it, the course did not become a strong selling point for prospective parents. On the surface, this decision-making process may sound feasible. However, what does the ropes course have to do with the climbing wall? Dorothy is honoring a sunk cost—the money put out for the ropes course three years ago—and allowing it to influence her current decision. A much better strategy would be to consider current assets and information. Does she have the money for the wall? What has been the experience of other camps with the wall? Does the supplier have information about effects of a wall on a camp's bottom line? Are there other "hot" items she could add instead? All of these considerations are much more likely to lead to a better decision than a comparison to an experience from three years ago.

2. *Decisions are based on the possible consequences of the choice.* This directly follows the avoidance of sunk costs in that only the future should be considered in making decisions. Imagine that for the past nine flips of a coin, tails had landed. If you were to bet on the

next flip, what would you choose? No matter how many times the coin consecutively lands on tails, on the next flip there still exists only a fifty-fifty chance that it will occur again. Basing a decision on past responses only would not necessarily be successful. We can look at the particulars of a past poor decision to improve our decisions in the present and future, but we should not discount a future alternative because the consequences of a similar past decision were disappointing. In the climbing wall example, it would be helpful to ask questions such as, "How could marketing of the tower be improved based on our marketing of the ropes course?" "Is the design of the wall well suited to the primary customer we seek to draw in?" Questions that look to the future include, "What are the advantages and disadvantages of adding a wall?" "What revenue could it bring to camp?" "What would be the financial result if the wall did not add to the camp's bottom line?" "Will the building of the wall necessarily take away from another possible improvement?" Such future considerations will obviously result in a better decision.

3. *If the possible consequences of a decision are uncertain, evaluate their likelihood according to the rules of probability.* This book is not meant as a primer on statistics and probability, so I cannot really cover these topics. However, a basic knowledge of probability theory can add greatly to rational decisions.

As an example, Terry is searching for a new secretary. The odds of finding a candidate with computer skills are greater than finding one with computer skills and accounting abilities. The addition of typing proficiency to computer and accounting skills even further reduces the odds that Terry will find a person with all the desired attributes. While this may sound obvious, people often want a successful outcome to have numerous attributes. However, the more attributes that are desired, the less probable a completely successful outcome is to occur. In short, as the number of desired attributes of any desired outcome increases, the likelihood of achieving that outcome decreases. The leader must determine the degree of influence that probability will be allowed to play in any given decision. The more critical the consequences of a decision, the less influence the leader should allow probability to have. In Terry's example, he will reduce the odds of finding the right employee by increasing the number of attributes he considers essential. He may end up with just the right person, but he may also have to make larger expenditures of resources to find that person. Is it any wonder that organizations put more resources toward hiring one CEO than they do toward hiring one entry-level position? As you look at the decisions you make, you will begin to see that probability does play a role in your decision-making strategies.

Solution 6: Try Problem Solving

There are a variety of ways that individuals cope with a problem. Some may choose the very first solution that occurs to them. Others will carefully map out numerous resolution methods. And some individuals may just ignore the problem in hopes that it will disappear. Again, each person has his or her preferred problem-solving method that is used repeatedly. Fortunately, some protocols for problem solving are very successful. We will look at the protocol of Seligman, which has five steps.

1. **Slow down**—Most problems do not need to be solved immediately. An impulsive response may do more damage than the original problem. The person involved would do best to remind him- or herself that a problem has occurred and that the following steps will be used to figure out a solution. Remember that problems are inevitable due to the randomness and uncertainty of life. Do not allow the cognitive distortion of exaggeration of a negative situation to rule judgment.

2. **Perspective taking**—This step is a necessity if another person is involved. Recall that cognitive distortions such as personalization and all or nothing thinking easily allow us to see another person as being completely at fault and acting purposefully. Are there any other possible interpretations for the person's behavior? Try to see the problem from the perspective of the other person. Ask the person if more information is necessary.

3. **Goal setting**—Some specific type of resolution of the problem is the ultimate goal. Once the person involved has decided on a goal, he or she can make a list of possible ways to achieve it. Many people recommend brainstorming any and all possible ways of achieving the goal, no matter how outlandish. Some people benefit from this technique, but others find it tedious. There is, however, usually more than just one way to reach the desired resolution.

4. **Considering consequences**—Once a person has formulated several methods to achieve the desired goal, it is essential to weigh both the advantages and disadvantages of each method. What are

the possible consequences if a particular solution is implemented? Particularly consider the effects of each method on other people.

5. **Executing**—Put the plan into action. If it works, then the problem is resolved. If it doesn't, return to step three and try again.

It is important to remember that many problems cannot be resolved immediately and that obstacles may arise to hinder progress toward the solution. Each obstacle can be considered a mini-problem on the way to the desired end solution. Remember that some of those obstacles will be random occurrences.

This chapter has introduced many of the obstacles to mental capacity as well as several solutions for their remediation. Unfortunately, as with much of psychology and medicine, we know more about the problems than about their solutions. If the leader is consecutively working on increasing the three capacities discussed thus far—physical, emotional, and mental—there will be positive changes in his or her abilities. The use of the feedback form at the conclusion of the book will help leaders recognize what characteristics employees believe would make the best leader. The change(s) a leader believes would be most beneficial may have little to do with the changes employees believe are necessary. A combination of desired personal change and input regarding change from others may be the best overall way to improve leadership.

Conclusion

Utilizing a variety of choice strategies will optimize your decision-making abilities and minimize the influence of cognitive distortions. In simple choices, such as which deodorant to purchase, the low-effort strategies would be adequate. The more complicated the choice, the more effort one should put into the strategy to be utilized. The previous list is not comprehensive, but it gives you a basic understanding of the options individuals have when making choices.

Refer to Workbook 5.9

Summary of Key Points

1. It is easier to change mental capacity than emotional capacity.
2. There are numerous obstacles to cognitive excellence. Three obstacles that have a profound influence are as follows.

- **Selective attention**—Humans have a limited awareness of all of the stimuli that affect us.
- **Cognitive limits**—The brain does not have unlimited abilities. The more it is used for one task, the less it is available for other tasks.
- **Speed over accuracy**—Quick decisions take precedence over accurate decisions.

3. Decision making, a major part of leadership, is made with cognitive shortcuts that affect success.

- **Memory**—Human beings make much use of information stored in their memory for decisions. What is remembered, however, may be very biased or selective.
- **Anchoring and adjust**—The first piece of information encountered, either in memory or as a factual piece of external information, may inadvertently become a starting point for decisions, even if the information is wrong.
- **Anchoring in the present**—How a person is thinking or feeling in the present manipulates recall of memory.
- **Similarity**—Decisions are made on the limited comparisons of similar attributes.
- **Randomness**—This entails making decisions based on patterns that are actually random events.

4. Cognitive distortions are immediate thoughts that affect emotions and behaviors. These immediate thoughts are often wrong.

- **All or nothing thinking**—A person interprets an event as extremely negative or positive.
- **Exaggeration of the positive or negative**—The importance of a pleasant or unpleasant event is greatly exaggerated.
- **Minimization**—The effects of a potentially serious consequence are underestimated.
- **Personalization**—Events appear personally directed at the individual.

5. Personal maps are our understanding of how the world is supposed to be. Several problems can occur with this.

- **Expectations guide perception**—Expectations focus what a person will pay attention to.

- **Expectations can lead to false memories**—A person can reconstruct the past so that it fits with his or her expectations.

6. There is more information available about cognitive capacity problems than about their solutions. Several solutions include the following.

- Make use of other people in formulating decisions.

- Learn data-sorting techniques to make the best use of available information.

- Accept randomness and uncertainty.

- Have variety in the strategies used for making choices.

- Have an understanding of rational decision making, including a basic knowledge of probability.

- Have an available problem-solving protocol.

CHAPTER 6

INTEGRATIVE FACTORS

Overview

Spiritual capacity is the most personal of the capacities, and it was originally understood as the use of values to define strong purposeful leadership. It would benefit leaders to evaluate their own goals and values. Psychology has only recently begun to thoroughly examine the effects of spirituality on well-being. The research that has arisen has been intriguing. The ongoing search for happiness in life, in contrast to well-being, is inevitably doomed to failure due to a combination of biological, evolutionary, and social factors. Instead, a person can seek well-being that will result in a happier and more satisfying life. The relatively new field of positive psychology has uncovered several means to achieve this.

[Yet, p]sychologists have scant knowledge of what makes life worth living. They have come to understand quite a bit about how people survive and endure under conditions of adversity. However, psychologists know very little about how normal people flourish under more benign conditions. Psychology has, since World War II, become a science largely about healing. It concentrates on repairing damage within a diseased model of human functioning. The almost exclusive attention to pathology neglects the fulfilled individual and the thriving community. The aim of positive psychology is to begin to catalyze a change in the focus of psychology from a preoccupation only with repairing the worst things in life to also building positive qualities.

Seligman and Csikszentmihalyi

Positive Psychology

Loehr and Schwartz, the creators of the high-performance pyramid, defined spiritual capacity as "tapping into one's deepest values and defining a strong sense of purpose" (p. 127). Knowledge of one's values and a sense of purpose is, however, a limited conceptualization in approaching spirituality. Unfortunately, psychological research on this topic is also quite limited, especially compared to the amount of information available on physical, emotional, and cognitive capacities. The same can be said for the field of anthropology, medicine, or any other field that may have a premise for studying spirituality. Empirical research is wanton. This can be explained in part by the object of attention in the concept of spirituality, that object being the spirit. If the spirit is an actual component of each human, it escapes direct observation. As such, the study of spirituality remains a study of the practices that arise out of holding to a view that humans have a spiritual component.

In an effort to bypass the paucity of research available on spirituality, this chapter will examine additional factors that did not quite have a place in the earlier chapters of the book. Thus, in addition to characteristics commonly associated with spirituality, such as faith, this chapter will explore other factors that may only be tangentially related to spirituality, such as optimism, and relationships.

This chapter, in order to reflect the material contained within, is called "Integrative Factors" instead of "Spiritual Capacity," as might be suggested by the high-performance pyramid. As such, consider this chapter my interpretation and expansion of the original high-performance pyramid. This cursory review of spiritual factors that influence leadership is not meant to detract from their importance. For many readers, the spiritual capacity of the performance pyramid will take precedence over all of the preceding levels.

Researchers in psychology, while sorely lacking in information on spiritual influences in life, have amassed a growing database about the achievement of happiness, satisfaction, and contentment in life. As the quote leading this chapter makes clear, psychology has focused much of its efforts on problems and cures. It has only been in the past several years that the topic of positive psychology has arisen. This new approach focuses on what is right with people and how to proliferate this knowledge so that others can begin to adapt similar strategies. Its goal is to make people stronger and more productive and to allow their potential to become active.

A cursory overview of the more recent studies in psychology will enable the reader to better understand the pioneering importance of positive psychology. Under the early influence of Freud, psychologists focused on internal and often unconscious experiences that affected each individual, almost always in a negative way. The behaviorist school, which followed, went to the exact opposite extreme. Internal experiences were considered immaterial. The behaviorist approach only studied what could be observed or measured. The internal life so prized by Freud was irrelevant because such experiences could not be formally analyzed. The next school of psychologists to develop was classified as humanist. These individuals focused on helping others reach a state of fulfillment and maximize their potential. While this in itself was important and quite a change from the dominant behaviorist school, it did not achieve its aims. In retrospect, it did not attract much research (a necessity for psychology) and, in many cases, focused on self-interest over the interests of the community and the world as a whole. We do have the humanist movement to thank for the myriad self-help books available in any bookstore, a direct outgrowth of the belief in maximizing one's potential. The final school on the scene was cognitive psychology. This branch of psychology examines how our thoughts and methods of thinking affect our lives. Much of the discussion in the chapter on mental capacity comes from this school, including topics such as problem solving, cognitive distortions, and cognitive limits. All of these developments in psychology have added enormously to the field. Techniques and research founded by each school are still in current use.

It is the humanist and cognitive schools that have paved the way for positive psychology. Thanks to the humanist school, we recognize that specific human traits, such as social support, empathy, and optimism, act as buffers against the numerous stressors of the world. This seemingly simple insight galvanized the prevention movement, which claims that if a person has a sufficient number of strengths, or buffers, he or she is less likely to get involved in unhealthy or dangerous behaviors, such as substance abuse and criminal acts. Prevention of negative involvements relies on maximizing an individual's strengths. The cognitive school espouses that people do indeed have control over their lives. Individuals are active decision makers and can make decisions that influence themselves for better or for worse. Both of these beliefs—that one can work on increasing specific strengths and that one has control over aspects of his or her life—have been discussed in this book. While genetics and our upbringing have influenced us in many ways that can never truly be altered, we still have sufficient control over ourselves to find contentment and satisfaction.

Obstacles to Happiness

While few would contest the statement that people seek happiness and contentment in their lives, there is no consensus on whether this is an appropriate goal in itself and, even more contentious, how to achieve this goal if it is appropriate. Psychological research has elucidated several obstacles to satisfaction in life that require clarification before the known factors that positively influence happiness can be introduced.

The first obstacle is the belief that, with enough effort, happiness is a state that can be permanently achieved. Recall the definition of an emotion from Chapter 4: An emotion is a temporary state. Happiness is an emotion. Therefore, happiness can only be temporary. Satisfaction is better classified as a mood. Moods, though longer lasting than emotions, are also temporary. Satisfaction is also a fleeting experience. Research agrees that intense positive emotions are rare experiences that last for only a brief period of time. These intense experiences can even be detrimental because an individual may use them as milestones on which to measure other aspects of his or her life. If a pleasant experience does not measure up to the intense happiness experienced in another situation, then the new experience is considered less satisfying. To conclude: happiness and satisfaction may be the goal of many individuals when, in actuality, they are experiences that are, by their very nature, temporary.

The second obstacle to happiness is our own biology. Our emotional set point plays a pivotal role in our attempts to maintain a level of happiness. People adapt to most conditions rather quickly. Silver found that persons with spinal cord injuries were very unhappy with their disability immediately after the accident. Within weeks, however, positive emotions began to take precedence over negative emotions. Other investigations have found similar results in other situations. For example, the emotional effects stemming from a variety of negative life events, such as being fired from a job, quickly diminish. This is not true for all negative experiences; for example, the loss of a loved one continues to produce negative emotions for an extended period of time for many people.

This adaptation to negative experiences also holds true for positive experiences. Lottery winners will experience intense pleasure at their luck. This quickly recedes, though, and within weeks the person is back to his or her emotional baseline or set point. Fortunately, most people appear to function in the mild to moderate pleasant range for their natural set point. In other words, humans are predisposed to have a generally pleasant emotional background experience when nothing bad is happening. Once again though, situations that evoke intense pleasant emotions will inevitably recede back to the mildly pleasant set point. So while external influences can and do have dramatic effects on emotional functioning, our genetic set point will likewise play just as big a role.

The third obstacle to happiness is that humans have survived as a species in part due to our ability to experience unhappiness and pain. We demonstrate certain traits that aided in the survival of our species. Imagine a person who could not experience any emotion but happiness. How long would he or she survive? A perpetually happy ancestor would not have had the required emotional repertoire for survival. For example, if he had encountered a wild animal, his lack of fear would not have galvanized him to make an effort to save his life. These perpetually happy individuals would have died off quickly.

Negative emotions are essential for survival in that they serve specific purposes. Jealousy is an apt example. It is an aid in the protection of an extremely valuable resource: one's mate. This emotion serves the same purpose today as it did for our ancestors. Other negative emotions, including anger, depression, anxiety, and fear, are all invaluable and built into the genes of each human being. And while all are essential and bound to occur on occasion, they all detract from happiness.

Another inborn trait is competitiveness. In a world with finite resources, not every living organism will survive. There are only a limited number of resources available for all existing creatures. For example, human beings have caused the extinction of innumerable species. This is as much a product of how we interact with our environment as it is a reflection on population growth. Ecology shows us that competition within a species plays a role in strengthening the species. The weak, the sick, and the lame are less likely to secure the necessary resources to survive. Consumptive interactions between species, that is eat or be eaten, play the same role but always within the bounds of ecological balance. This means that any surviving member of any species stems from a long line of ancestors who were successful in one way or another in competition for limited resources. One unfortunate result of this was nicely summed up by Buss: "The profound implication of this…is that humans have evolved psychological mechanisms designed to inflict costs on others, to gain advantage at the expense of others, to delight in the downfall of others, and to envy those who are more successful at achieving their goals toward which they aspire" (p. 18).

Shelton (2001) described the effects of competition in camp when several people were aiming for promotion to a new position. The promotion can be looked at as a finite resource, because only one person can be successful. Those not promoted would be expected to demonstrate negative reactions that, while damaging to the camp environment, are sensible from a competitive standpoint. These emotions may include envy, avoidance of the promoted individual, denigration of the promoted person's reputation, and active interference with that person's new duties. If we accept this point of view, then we must recognize that other people will occasionally attempt to thwart the achievement of our own goals and our resulting satisfaction. The reverse is true. We will often experience envy when we encounter people who are more successful than we are. The success of one person often equates with a loss for another. The emotion of envy prepares a person to save his or her own self-esteem.

The implications for this are dramatic. As one potential leader wins at the perceived expense of others that leader's first challenge may very well be to deal with those who harbor envy, display avoidance, or publicly denigrate the successful leader. From this comes the practice of cleaning house when a corporate takeover or restructuring occurs. New top leadership is put in place, and middle management is released. Those further down are promoted to the vacant middle management positions. The new leadership releases those who might derail their efforts while at the same time setting themselves up as heroes for the new middle management. The new middle management will let go of their bad feelings about the restructuring for the sake of securing and keeping their higher positions. A rare individual will forsake these management tactics for personal ideals. That is, once they are promoted they will usually not walk away from the promotion to protest the restructuring tactics—at least not until they have secured a contingency plan.

There are many other ways to minimize contention about your opportunity to lead, but the example cited above is a familiar one. What is surprising, and hard to swallow, especially if you have been on the receiving end of such a restructuring, is that in some business environments, cleaning house is the best way to advance leadership and minimize contention with that leadership.

Another important human trait is that the pain associated with a loss is more intense than the pleasure associated with a gain. A person who loses $100, for example, experiences more displeasure than the pleasure he or she experiences after winning of the same amount. This evolutionary holdout likely developed because those individuals who felt a keen sense of loss would be more careful in protecting their property, including food, money, or shelter. The end result is that we now have more profound emotions of loss as compared to pleasure. If one can recall the observation from the very beginning of this book, there are many more negative emotions than positive emotions. Each emotion, whether positive or negative, serves a purpose. It is probably the negative emotions that did the most to ensure the ongoing survival of our species. Therefore, we are certain to have more variances from our emotional set point that are negative than that are positive over the course of a lifetime.

Another insight gained from the perspective of adaptation is that the environmental conditions of modern man may negatively affect happiness. Humans have lived throughout most of their history in small groups of fifty to two hundred individuals. They lived in a network of extended kin. They may have had only two dozen possible mating partners to choose from. Today, most people live in an environment surrounded by thousands or millions of other people, and we are often removed from our kin. This variety in friends and partners may seem superficially beneficial, but problems quickly arise. For instance, men exposed to multiple images of attractive females rated their commitment to their present partners as lower in comparison to men who saw neutral images. Women, similarly, showed a decrease in commitment to their partners when shown images of high-status males. Both these findings indicate that modern life with its barrage of contact with other people, both in real life and through the media, can detract from happiness by leading to dissatisfaction with current partners. Furthermore, increased contact with other people also leads to more situations in which envy is a possible reaction. "In the ancestral environment you would have had a good chance at being the best at something. Even if you were not the best, your group would likely value your skills. Now we all compete with those who are the best in the world. Watching these successful people on television arouses envy… Now few of us can achieve the goals envy sets for us, and none can attain the fantasy lives we see on television" (Nesse and Williams, p. 220).

Modern living conditions also reduce the social support that was available to our ancestors in their intimately shared environments. While the quantity of available and realized social connections may have increased, the quality of those connections has decreased. Superficial and short-term social connections have replaced formative long-term relationships. This is true whether we are talking about an intimate partner or the town grocer. The epitome of this is electronic chat rooms where social connections can be born, live, and die all in one evening. Certainly such forums have the potential for positive impact, but they are poor replacements for long-term, in-person, formative social engagement. There is a growing realization that the reduction in ties and connections so prevalent today may be one of the associated causes of mental illness, and therefore it is yet another reason for difficulty in achieving well-being and satisfaction.

There is one final obstacle to happiness. Many people believe that money can buy happiness. Consider the following facts.

- In a 1981 survey by Campbell asking what would improve the quality of participants' lives, the most frequent response was more money.

- In a 1984 poll by the Roper Organization asking participants about satisfaction with different aspects of their lives, Americans expressed the least satisfaction with the amount of money they had to live on.

- A Gallup poll found that one in two women, two in three men, and four in five people earning more than $75,000 reported that they wanted to be rich.

- A survey by Sax, Astin, Korn, and Mahoney of almost a quarter of a million students entering college reported that three out of four believed that the ability to make more money was a very important reason for going to college. This objective was ranked as number one out of a list of nineteen and superseded other possible goals including raising a family and developing a meaningful philosophy of life.

All of the above surveys point to the belief that life would be improved if a person only had more money. The connection between happiness and wealth has fortunately not been lost in psychology. Researchers have examined this particular association and come up with some sobering and often surprising conclusions.

The most relevant finding is that there is no increase in subjective well-being that comes with increased wealth. "Now…it is becoming clear that the…inhabitants of the wealthiest industrialized Western nations are living in a period of unprecedented riches, in conditions that previous generations would have considered luxuriously comfortable, in relative peace and security, and they are living on the average close to twice as long as their grandparents did. Yet, despite all these improvements in material conditions, it does not seem that people are so much more satisfied with their lives than they were before" (Csikszentmihalyi, p. 822).

Sociological studies have examined whether happiness increases along with wealth. In 1957, the average income, expressed in today's dollars, was approximately $9,000. It is currently twice that amount. Americans now have "twice as many cars per person, eat out more than twice as often, and often enjoy microwave ovens, big-screen color TVs, and home computers" (Myers, p. 61). In contrast, the number of people reporting themselves as very happy has not only failed to keep pace with the advancement in wealth but has actually declined slightly. The results of the research indicate that, though we may be twice as wealthy, we are in no way happier. While there is a tendency for wealthier nations to have more satisfied people in comparison to poorer nations, there appears to be little difference in satisfaction levels when the gross national product reaches $8,000 per person. Money provides diminishing returns on happiness.

Studies of very wealthy individuals have not found dramatic differences in their happiness levels. The very rich appear to be only slightly happier than the average American is. On a case by case example, there are rich individuals who are exceedingly unhappy and others who are very happy. This is similar to the happiness levels of the average-income American.

Csikszentmihalyi formulated four major reasons for the finding that happiness is not strongly associated with wealth. The first utilizes the concept of adaptation once again. Recall that humans quickly adapt to most situations, whether positive or negative, and return to their basic emotional functioning level. The same holds true for financial security. If a person strives for a certain level of affluence, he or she finds that, upon reaching it, adaptation will occur. The individual quickly adjusts to the new level of income and becomes desirous of obtaining the next highest level. Few people are ever satisfied for very long with what they have.

The second reason relates to the first. Growing disparity in wealth makes even an affluent person consider herself poor. Humans do not base their satisfaction levels on what they currently possess or what they even really need. Instead they compare themselves to those who have more. Since the income disparity between the very rich and everybody else continues to grow with each passing year, it appears as if the use of this group as a comparison to measure personal satisfaction level will continue to dictate the need for more wealth and material goods. On a much more local scale "keeping up with the Joneses" is a very real phenomenon. A neighborhood is impacted when a family leaves for a nicer neighborhood, parks a new motor home in their driveway, broadcasts a significant job promotion, or announces the acceptance of a child at an Ivy League school. These events become a point of admiration and perhaps even trigger dissatisfaction with one's own station in life. Each event has financial implications.

The third reason is that as more and more effort is put into obtaining wealth, there is less time to pursue other objectives and goals. "Material advantages do not readily translate into social and emotional benefits. In fact, to the extent that most of one's psychic energy becomes invested in material goods, it is typical for sensitivity to other rewards to atrophy. Friendship, art, literature, natural beauty, religion, and philosophy become less and less interesting" (Csikszentmihalyi, p. 823). Because time is considered a commodity, and individuals attempt to maximize the use of their time, the more time that is spent in the pursuit of wealth, the less there is available for other, possibly more satisfying endeavors.

Finally, since most aspects of life are now measured in dollars, there are fewer and fewer activities available that do not have some measurable financial benefit. Historians have documented that in the past there was a much greater variety of lifestyles a person could emulate. Nowadays the marker of success and happiness is the amount of wealth a person achieves. As more and more people seek wealth, these alternative lifestyles are valued less and less. The end result is that the number of different cultural options for finding happiness is rapidly diminishing. Thus, instead of finding lifelong satisfaction in a career, as people in the past often did, we now choose activities and interests that will fetch the most income.

The cumulative result of all of these findings is that not only does increased wealth rarely result in increased happiness, but, quite the reverse, it can make a person less satisfied with life. Thus the belief that money can increase happiness is deeply flawed. After reaching a certain threshold of wealth, more material goods do not make much of a difference in relative happiness.

This section has introduced four obstacles to happiness. (1) We mistakenly believe that happiness is a permanent state that can somehow be achieved. (2) Our biology will influence our happiness and satisfaction, especially as it adapts to pleasant emotions. (3) In evolutionary terms, we have developed so as to experience distress and unpleasant emotions. (4) Many believe that money is the root of happiness. Happiness and contentment, though the ultimate goals for the great majority of the world, are exceedingly transient and difficult to achieve. With this information now out of the way, we can begin to look at the factors that do positively influence happiness and satisfaction levels in life.

The Building Blocks of Psychological Well-Being

Since it is clear that happiness is a short-term emotional state at best, psychologists have undertaken an investigation of what constitutes long-term psychological well-being. It may be that people who have achieved this level experience more moments of happiness. The actual definition of psychological well-being is still in the process of clarification. Many different definitions have been offered, but none have been accepted by all. In the most simplistic form, well-being is the absence of distress. Psychological well-being is certainly more than this, though, just as health is more than the absence of sickness.

There is more agreement on the actual characteristics that add up to long-term well-being. The following pages will examine several of the most pertinent characteristics.

Optimism—Optimism is linked to many desirable and beneficial characteristics including happiness, achievement, health, and perseverance. Optimism consists of both cognitive and emotional aspects. In the cognitive sense, optimism is experienced as a positive expectation about future occurrences. Emotionally, optimism is experienced as a positive emotion or mood associated with a thought. Most of the research has focused on the cognitive aspects of this particular characteristic of psychological well-being. This is true of almost all psychological research since, as stated in the chapter on emotional capacity, emotions have only recently received significant attention.

Optimism has been approached in terms of an individual's characteristic explanatory style. The way a person explains bad events is the defining quality between optimism and lack of optimism. Optimistic individuals have an explanatory style that interprets negative events as circumscribed by saying, "This is a bad event, but it doesn't affect all areas of my life"; as temporary by saying, "I just need to get through this and everything will be all right"; and as external by saying, "It's not all my fault." Let's see how Aaron would interpret an event at his camp with an optimistic explanatory style.

Aaron was on duty for his group of campers one evening while the remainder of his co-counselors were in town. He heard several of the campers in one cabin laughing. Aaron stood outside the window and told them to go to sleep. This happened on several occasions over the next hour. It was only the next morning that it was discovered that the group of campers had joined together to cover another sleeping child in the cabin with shaving cream, deodorant, and toothpaste.

Aaron's optimistic interpretation: "I screwed up. I should have gone into the cabin and checked when I heard their laughing. I won't let that happen again (temporary thought). I told the director that we shouldn't place Michael and Donald in the same cabin (external thought). Hopefully the fact that I do such a great job at the talent show will stop the director from getting too angry (circumscribed thought)."

Conversely, pessimistic individuals explain bad events as permanent by saying, "It's going to last forever"; as personal by saying, "It's my fault"; and as pervasive by saying, "Everything's ruined now." In other words, a pessimistic individual interprets negative experiences as lasting forever, affecting everything, and reflecting personal failings. **Aaron's pessimistic interpretation:** "I'm going to get fired now. This is the last time they'll let me work at this camp (pervasive thought). I'll never be able to work with kids (permanent thought). I'm such an idiot. I should have known better (personal thought)."

As the chapters on cognitive and emotional capacities made clear, events are interpreted in the brain. Optimistic and pessimistic individuals demonstrate consistent but different patterns of interpretation. Optimistic individuals don't immediately place sole responsibility for a negative event on themselves. Neither do they see it as affecting every aspect of their lives. They see that the negative event affects some things but not everything. Finally, they do not interpret the event as lasting forever. Optimism must, of course, be tempered with reality. An individual who commits horrible acts yet places the blame for them on others may be an optimistic person but certainly is also psychologically unhealthy. However, the same applies to pessimists. While they may do a great job at accepting responsibility for their faults, they may go overboard and accept responsibility for events they have absolutely no control over. Recall that acceptance of the randomness of life is one of the necessities of sound leadership. If a leader continually accepts responsibility for events that she had no control over, capable leadership is bound to suffer.

Pessimistic thinking results in a belief that the involved individual has little control over outcomes. His or her actions will have little effect on the future. Optimistic thinking results in a belief in the ability to change outcomes and to be an active agent in one's own life. Fortunately, people can learn to increase optimistic thinking. The main skill has already been covered in the chapter on mental capacity: disputation. Automatically pessimistic thoughts that arise during or after a negative event need to be evaluated for their basis in reality and, if necessary, disputed with more realistic thinking. Like any other skill, the more effort a person puts into recognizing and disputing automatic thoughts, the less effort it will take to perform the same task as time goes on. The disputation of automatic thoughts of permanence, pervasiveness, and personal blame will lead to increased optimistic thinking.

Refer to Workbook 6.1

Hope–Hope is a concept similar to optimism. Psychological formulations of this concept have focused less on optimistic versus pessimistic explanatory styles and more on the belief that one's goals can be achieved.

C. R. Snyder, one of the preeminent researchers on the topic, states that hope consists of two separate variables. The first is personal agency—the belief that one's goal can be achieved. The second is the belief that plans can be generated to reach such goals. While optimism and hope both share a belief in personal agency, or the personal ability to change an outcome, hope focuses more on the belief that there are methods to resolve a problem. Hopeful individuals have been found to have higher self-esteem, to experience more positive emotions, and to achieve their goals more often.

Relationships—Humans developed in small groups. One of the reasons for the survival of the species was the ability to get along with other people. "[S]ocial and evolutionary psychologists remind us that we are…social animals. Social bonds boosted our ancestors' survival chances. Children that kept close to their caregivers were protected from harm. Adults who formed attachments were more likely to come together to reproduce and conurture their offspring to maturity. Groups shared food, provided mates, and helped care for children…As inheritors of this legacy, we therefore have a deep need to belong" (Myers, p. 62).

Such an inherent human need is the likely reason for the finding that close relationships predict physical health. For example, people who have close relationships are less vulnerable to health problems and premature death. In regard to psychological well-being, individuals with close relationships cope better with both minor and major stressors. They also report more moments of happiness and satisfaction. Studies of individuals in satisfying marriages indicate that they are happier than those who are divorced, separated, or never married. There is, therefore, a general consensus that relationships are a major component of psychological well-being.

Faith—Evidence abounds that participation in religious activity has many benefits, including fewer instances of divorce, less drug and alcohol use, and less antisocial behavior. In addition, individuals who are active in their faith tend to be physically healthier and live longer. In regard to emotional well-being, such people report more instances of joy and happiness, are less depressed, and are more satisfied with their lives. There is no scientifically proven reason that faith has such positive effects, but then again we may be discussing a reality that is beyond today's scientific rigor. Some surmise that the connection between faith and health occurs because faith communities provide social support. Others believe that faith gives a sense of meaning and purpose to existence, which in turn results in the improvements stated above. A third idea is that faith encourages people to have hope, which, as shown earlier, is already associated with well-being. A final possibility is that participation in a religious life leads to a higher level of satisfaction because a religious life is part of our design. Humans do best when their environment includes an expression of faith because we are designed to realize a spiritual life.

Motivation–Researchers in human motivation have discovered much valuable information for leaders. At just about every camp conference there is a workshop on motivating employees. Many of these sessions focus on a system of rewards that help increase positive behaviors of camp staff. While there is nothing wrong with this approach, such an intervention only begins to scratch the surface of the science of motivation.

Motivation can be broken down into two separate components: intrinsic motivation and extrinsic motivation. Intrinsic motivation occurs when an individual participates in an activity for the challenge or enjoyment of it. "Perhaps no single phenomenon reflects the positive potential of human nature as much as intrinsic motivation, the inherent tendency to seek out novelty and challenges, to extend and exercise one's capacities, to explore, and to learn" (Ryan and Deci, p. 70). Extrinsic motivation, in contrast, focuses on involvement in a task in order to attain a separate outcome. This type of motivation results from variables other than personal enjoyment, such as the aspiration toward reward or the avoidance of punishment. As an example, many people dislike their job but continue to work simply because it brings a paycheck. These individuals find no satisfaction in the job; it is the reward of the paycheck that motivates them.

Intrinsic motivation occurs naturally in children. They are inquisitive and curious, and they participate in challenging activities without the need for external rewards. As individuals mature into adults, however, there are fewer and fewer opportunities to participate in intrinsically motivating activities. Adults conform to social pressures to participate in less interesting activities and to assume more responsibilities.

Leaders are faced with numerous tasks and responsibilities that have a high potential to generate boredom and frustration. Even worse, leaders may have to participate in activities that are actually feared or abhorred, such as giving a presentation to a board of directors. In such cases the leader is not intrinsically motivated to complete the duties, because he or she receives no internal joy or satisfaction from their completion. The external threats of losing business due to delayed paperwork or facing the scowls of a displeased board are the motivating factors.

Psychological well-being incorporates both types of motivation. Individuals need to be able to motivate themselves to perform activities that they do not want to participate in. This is the common theme of most conference sessions on motivation–how to reward oneself and staff in order to achieve desired results. Even more important, though, is the recognition of the profound influence of intrinsic motivation. People who foster this type of motivation continually challenge themselves, seek mastery over obstacles, and have higher levels of enjoyment and satisfaction in life. This particular aspect of intrinsic motivation will be explored in the upcoming section on flow.

Social environments also affect motivation. This is particularly important for camp professionals because the camp environment affects not only the designated leader but also the staff and the campers they supervise. While it is currently impossible to make somebody intrinsically interested in an activity, it is possible to influence extrinsic motivation. Intrinsic motivation is a personal matter; a person either enjoys something or he doesn't. A camp leader can introduce campers and staff to numerous new and possibly challenging activities but cannot make any participant like that activity. On the other hand, the leader can reduce the reliance on externally motivating factors to ensure participation. Extrinsic motivation exists along a continuum. At one end is a complete reliance on external threats or rewards to force involvement. At the other end is acceptance of an activity as valuable, though not particularly pleasant. Exercise involvement is a good example. Most individuals do not find participation in an exercise regimen a pleasant experience nor is it one that they gleefully look forward to. However, it is possible to move the person from thinking that exercise is strictly to avoid health problems (a threat) to thinking that exercise is a valuable contribution to overall well-being.

Example

This example is taken directly from my own camp experience. As a unit leader for a group of twenty-eight boys, it was my responsibility to coordinate an overnight camping trip for each new group of children that arrived. The staff that worked with me hated this event, and they only participated because they had to, since job-related consequences could occur if they refused. Their participation was due strictly to the lowest form of extrinsic motivation. As the staff and I worked together over the season, they witnessed firsthand the beneficial effects of the camping trip on the relationships among the campers. The trip appeared to bond them to each other and to the counselors. After the trip, they noticed that campers were easier to manage and that they themselves could interact more comfortably, allowing them to step down from a disciplinary role. So although the staff never reached a point of intrinsic motivation for the overnight outing (and probably never would), they did begin to appreciate its effects and value at least the purpose of the trip.

It is clear that extrinsic motivation can be positively influenced in environments that allow participants to experience competence in new activities and to maintain some type of autonomy in the decision. In my camp example, I galvanized my staff's interests by allowing them to choose the exact date of each trip and the location of the campsite (autonomy). Since they had no choice but to go on the trip, I attempted to place as much autonomy into the outing as possible. In addition, each staff member was responsible for one new duty on every camping trip so that each acquired more competence with leading a camp outing as a whole.

Leaders can increase their ability to perform tasks that are strictly extrinsically motivated by building autonomy and competence into them. Thus, while they may never enjoy certain activities, they can at least reach a point where they cease to rely strictly on rewards or fears of consequences to motivate themselves. Extrinsic motivations facilitate a process of adaptation.

Flow—Flow, a term popularized by Mihaly Csikszentmihalyi, has been shrugged off by many as simply another self-help gimmick. However, the concept has strong psychological support. It occurs when a person loses himself in an activity that is intrinsically motivating. Csikszentmihalyi is careful to separate out the common understanding of "going with the flow" from his findings. In the former, the participant abandons himself or herself to an experience that feels good. In the latter psychological interpretation of flow, there is a requirement of concentration, perseverance, and skill. Csikszentmihalyi himself summed it up best when he wrote "people are happy not because of what they do, but because of how they do it" (p. 826).

A flow experience is one that thoroughly engrosses an individual. Such experiences usually consist of the following characteristics. First, they are separate from the routines of daily life. Second, involvement is so intense that the world surrounding the participant becomes irrelevant, and attention is so focused on the activity that little is left for additional scrutiny. Finally, the activity appears to require little effort on the part of the participant even though it might be quite challenging.

Individuals who have moments of flow report more positive states and find their lives more meaningful. Flow does not require wealth or material goods. It only requires the ability to get fully involved in an activity that matches the skills of the participant. In the context of this book, flow would be equivalent to the dedication of a sufficient percentage of emotional, mental, and physical capacities to a given task so that anything outside the present task is considered a distraction. Intense flow may create a situation where all capacities are so engaged that outside events are simply not noticed and internal events may even become muted. The individual simply has no more capacity to accommodate any additional input from the external or internal environment. Interestingly, it follows that those who have higher capacities would have to engage in a correspondingly more complex and engaging task to experience flow.

Flow, of course, does not create a happy life, but it does enable individuals to experience a more satisfied existence.

Although a permanent state of happiness and satisfaction is impossible, this section has introduced factors that can lead to more happy and more satisfied lives. Optimism, hope, relationships, faith, participation in intrinsically motivating activities, and moments of flow all augment long-term psychological well-being. Fortunately, the experiences that increase this well-being also aid in increased happiness and satisfaction.

All of these can be incorporated into the life of a leader. He can begin to dispute pessimistic thoughts so as to become a more optimistic thinker. She can increase social ties and involvement in a community of faith. Purposefully taking time to participate in challenging, intrinsically motivating activities will increase moments of flow. And why is all of this important? As has been stated several times throughout this book, the leader has an enormous influence on his or her employees and on the organization as a whole. A leader who is happier and satisfied will instill this throughout the workplace. The satisfied camp leader will have satisfied employees. They in turn will have satisfied campers. All of this results in a satisfied and happier camp.

Refer to Workbook 6.2

Know Thyself

Camp leaders live in a perpetual state of triage. Problems, obstacles, and the occasional emergency occur with enough regularity (particularly during the summer season) to prevent the leader from examining his or her own goals and aspirations carefully. As if this weren't enough, there is difficulty for everybody in knowing what constitutes a "good life," since so much of our activity is measured in monetary value.

With the barrage of conflicting and often negative societal messages combined with the lack of time so common to leaders, it is difficult to establish one's values. This is essential though. There are several ways to begin this self-reflection, including the use of the feedback tool presented in Chapter 7. The leader can meditate, maintain a journal, pray, or perform volunteer service. The most important ingredient, though, is time. If a leader does not take sufficient time to understand himself or herself, then excellence in leadership will never be achieved.

Refer to Workbook 6.3

Level 5 Leadership

Collins released the results of a five-year study that examined one specific question: Can a good company become a great one? He and his associates looked at companies that had shifted from good performance to sustained great performance. The data utilized for this decision were based on stock market returns. Companies were chosen that had returns at or below the general stock market for fifteen years and then had a sudden transition to three times the market for the following fifteen years. Specific parameters made sure that the growth was not associated merely with changes in an entire industry. In other words, if the entire computer industry showed a dramatic transition, individual companies that composed this industry were not included in the study. The study was seeking to discover what factors in a single company were responsible for the shift from unremarkable to fantastic.

While this study examined publicly traded companies, the results are just as salient for small organizations, including camps and retreats. Although the researchers had entered into the study with suppositions regarding the catalyst(s) for the dramatic change, they were unprepared for the result. The most important factor in the positive transition was the leader of the company. "The executives at companies that went from good to great and sustained that performance for fifteen years or more were all cut from the same cloth—one remarkably different from that which produced executives at the comparison companies in our study. It didn't matter whether the company was in crisis or steady state, consumer or industrial, offering services or products. It didn't matter when the transition took place or how big the company" (Collins, p. 70).

This finding showed that it was the leader who made the largest contribution in a company's strikingly dramatic shift from merely acceptable to outstanding. Each person reading this book is probably attempting to increase his or her leadership abilities and therefore an organization as a whole. This research finding is proof that not only is it possible for a leader to make a dramatic difference in a company, but with the right principles and drive, incredible change is in the realm of possibility. Even if level 5 leadership does prove to be above the capabilities of most leaders, each advancement in leadership strength will nevertheless result in a stronger organization. The results are unequivocal: Leaders make the difference.

Summary of Key Points

1. Psychology has focused much of its past efforts on problems and cures. It has only been in the past several years that the topic of positive psychology has arisen. This new approach focuses on what is right with people. Its goal is to make people stronger and more productive and to allow their potential to become active.

2. Psychology has elucidated four major obstacles to a permanent state of happiness.

   - Happiness and satisfaction are transient by their very nature.
   - Due to our genetic make-up, we will both adapt quickly to happiness and return to our emotional set point.
   - Distress and negative emotions have evolved in our species to serve specific purposes.
   - The belief that money can buy happiness, while deeply entrenched, is incorrect.

3. Individuals with emotional well-being will have happier and more satisfying lives.

4. Several factors have been shown to contribute to emotional well-being.

   - Optimism
   - Hope
   - Relationships
   - Faith
   - Motivation
   - Flow

5. Because camp leaders live in a perpetual state of triage with numerous problems, obstacles, and occasional emergencies, they rarely have the time to explore their own personal goals. It would benefit them greatly to take time to examine themselves in order to make decisions and to live a life that is in agreement with their defined values and purpose.

CHAPTER 7

PERSONAL CHANGE

Overview

Change can be difficult. Individuals face myriad challenges when they attempt to implement change. Change is best looked at as an ongoing long-term process rather than as an all-or-nothing event. One valuable change for leaders is to improve upon traditional evaluation methods. The more input a leader has from different sources, such as employees or peers, the more likely he or she will benefit from the evaluation and know which self-improvements are most necessary.

Evaluations

You may already know about some of your weak areas. Throughout the reading of this text, you may have found more areas for improvement. However, introspection and self-evaluation cannot give the complete picture. Other people are necessary for a comprehensive evaluation.

A person's supervisor performs the traditional evaluation. Leaders may not actually report directly to anybody, thus forfeiting this possible input of valuable information. But even if you do have some person that you must report to, there is still one major problem with this type of evaluation: this person only sees you in a circumscribed set of situations. We may act very differently around our boss than we do around our coworkers or our employees. While the person performing an evaluation on a leader is certainly attempting to be as accurate and thorough as possible, this individual still only knows some facets of the leader. Other people have valuable information and feedback as well.

Coworkers and peers have evolved opinions about the leader's strengths and weaknesses. Peers may be uncomfortable, though, about giving any type of feedback that is the least bit negative. Employees, on the other hand, would be right to have trepidation, if not outright fear, regarding the presentation of negative feedback to their leader. The challenge is to find a way of eliciting feedback from these major sources of valuable information, the boss, peers, and employees.

Many large organizations, including the majority of the Fortune 500 companies, have recognized the limited value of the traditional evaluation process. Many now use a 360-degree performance appraisal system. Instead of a single evaluation, an appraisal includes multiple sources of feedback. The boss still gives feedback, but so do peers and employees. This collection of multiple perspectives comprises the final evaluation. A brief description of the process is as follows.

- Involved individuals complete anonymous surveys.
- Data from the surveys are formulated into an overall report on the leader.
- The leader meets with his or her supervisor to discuss the results and plan for future development.

There are benefits for all participants that do not come from more traditional evaluations.

- **The leader**—This individual receives a far more accurate and well-rounded evaluation of performance. This allows him or her to formulate a better plan for self-improvement.
- **Peers and employees**—Such evaluations improve teamwork and the ability to work together more productively since concerns are brought into the open.
- **A leader's supervisor**—The process allows a more comprehensive picture of the leader than one based on the few interactions they have together.

All of these improvements will result in not only a stronger leader and better relationships within the organization but also a stronger organization as a whole.

Each 360-degree evaluation measures different characteristics. In general, though, the evaluations measure similar competencies, including leadership skills, management skills, quality of work, teamwork, adaptability, staff development skills, communication skills, and knowledge of the field. The evaluation addresses specific behaviors indicative of each competency.

Although there are no claims that 360-degree evaluations are perfect, they are far better than traditional methods, provided that the methodology is well conceived and implemented. Several concerns have become evident as these evaluations become more common. One such concern is whether the evaluation is to be used for developmental purposes or for decisions regarding compensation, usually raises. Another is that without proper introduction of the evaluation into an organization, staff members may respond with reluctance and even resistance. A 360-degree evaluation is not a one-time occurrence. It is meant to occur on a regular basis so as to indicate success or lack of success regarding specific changes. Employees are appropriately skeptical if they complete such an evaluation and then never see any tangible change. However, there are several reasons that many companies do not make use of this process. They may lack the knowledge to implement the process. Their current business culture rejects the process. Or, those who coordinate and participate in the evaluation process simply do not have the time to handle the increased commitment of a 360-degree evaluation process.

Supervisors often recognize that their evaluation method is not satisfactory, but they do not know what to substitute in its place. Camp and retreat leaders who have, up to now, not known of such a tool can begin to consider its value for their organizations. Following is an evaluation method that camp and retreat leaders can use that has proven successful for many such businesses.

A Camp and Retreat Director Evaluation

There are numerous 360-degree feedback evaluations available. A cursory search on the Internet will find a multitude of organizations offering this service. Some require a thorough orientation, while others simply request some basic information to prepare the survey. The number of examined characteristics fluctuates from one evaluation to another. Some look at just a few executive qualities. Others evaluate almost one hundred different characteristics. While many variations are available, there is no reason why a small facility cannot create its own 360-degree evaluation. Many small or independent companies have successfully done just this.

The evaluation form shown on pages 173–176 for camp and retreat directors will utilize the basic format of a 360-degree feedback device but in a less complicated form. Many of the evaluations available require some knowledge of statistical analysis. This particular evaluation will require no such knowledge base. The evaluation is meant simply to collect feedback from the leader's boss, if such a person exists, and from peers and employees, known as direct reports in the evaluation business. The leader will perform a personal evaluation and then compare the personal results with the combined tally of the other participants in the process.

Before the evaluation process is even initiated, the leader must prepare for the results. If participants are honest, there is bound to be some critical feedback. Therefore, it is important to decide who will work with the leader not only to make sense of the feedback but also to assist in desired change. The last section of this chapter will focus on implementing personal change. But as an introduction, the process of change is filled with obstacles. Successful long-term change will be more complicated without a support person. A leader who attempts to implement change without such assistance has a reduced chance of success. If the leader has a person who actually supervises him or her, this is the ideal person to involve in the change process. If the leader is the top person and has nobody that he or she reports to, now is the time to begin considering who might offer such assistance. A trusted director of another facility is one example. Once again, the leader can certainly go it alone but may find the challenges overpowering.

The following is an overview of the evaluation process.

- The leader will pick between twelve and fifteen peers and employees to complete the anonymous survey. If the leader has direct access to these participants and knows that they will complete the evaluation, the lower number of participants will be used. If the leader must elicit the support of seasonal employees, the larger number will be used. This is because some evaluations will not be completed and returned. If all participants do return the form to the leader, there is certainly no harm done, and there is more feedback available.

- Evaluations will be distributed through the mail with a cover letter explaining its purpose and a self-addressed stamped envelope. The entire evaluation should take no more than fifteen minutes to complete.

- The leader will personally complete the evaluation prior to having access to the feedback from anyone else who participates in the process.

- The leader's supervisor completes an evaluation.

- Returned evaluations will be kept sealed until at least eighty percent have been returned. If the leader opens them as they arrive, there is the possibility of an emotional roller coaster as each one is taken at face value.

- Upon the arrival of the majority of the evaluations, the results will be tabulated (don't worry, this will be simple) and compared to the self-evaluation the leader performed.

- The leader will discuss the results with his or her designated boss or supervisor and make decisions regarding desired change(s).
- The leader thanks participants for their assistance, preferably in written form.

Any feedback will be of limited value if the participants think that they risk repercussions for their honest involvement. There are two strategies for minimizing the effect of this concern. Both will be clearly stated in the letter accompanying the tool. The first is that the feedback device is anonymous. Although the leader does know the specific peers and employees that were asked to participate, he or she will be unable to separate one particular response from another. The second precaution is to clearly state the purpose of this procedure. It is not a process of searching for dissatisfied employees but rather to improve the performance of the leader. The only participant whose identity will not be kept hidden is the leader's supervisor, if applicable. The supervisor is expected to give ongoing honest feedback.

The leader will do more damage if he or she attempts to learn the identity of specific responders. **If the leader knows that unpleasant feedback will end in a hunt for those who were critical in their evaluations, then please do not use the tool.** It is imperative that responders are not punished for their feedback for this process to have any value.. Concerns and emotions brought up in the process should be discussed with a supervisor or a person chosen specifically to assist in leadership development.

In order to obtain the best information, the leader should not stack the deck by sending out evaluations only to those who like him or her. The leader should choose a wide spectrum of associations including peers and employees with whom he or she has established strong relationships and others with whom this is lacking. The only requirement is that each person has worked with the leader for enough time to be aware of his or her weaknesses. "Work with" does not necessarily mean in the same organization. If, for example, the leader assisted in facilitating a workshop with another camp leader, this person may have valuable feedback.

The following is a recommended breakdown of participants.

1. Leaders who have a largely seasonal staff
   - One self-evaluation
   - One evaluation completed by the leader's supervisor, if applicable
   - Three evaluations completed by peers, for example, those in similar positions either in the same organization or other camps and retreats

- Eleven evaluations completed by seasonal employees
2. Leaders who maintain a regular year-round staff
   - One self-evaluation
   - One evaluation completed by the leader's supervisor, if applicable
   - Two evaluations completed by peers, for example, those in similar positions either in the same organization or other camps and retreats
   - Nine evaluations completed by a combination of year-round and seasonal employees

Evaluations will be mailed out with a self-addressed stamped envelope, because the less effort that is required of the respondent, the more likely the evaluation will be completed and returned. While it might be easier to hand out evaluations to available employees, their sense of anonymity will be fostered through the use of the mail.

The following is a sample cover letter. The leader can simply copy it and add in his or her own information or rewrite it to match a personal style. There are three major points to be made in the letter no matter how it is formulated.

- The anonymity of the participant
- The reason for the evaluation
- The brief amount of time it will take to complete it

Most people would have a tough time ignoring an honest request such as that represented in the letter.

Enclose the cover letter with the evaluation tool on pages 173–176 and mail them off. Then give a copy of the evaluation to your supervisor for completion. Finally, complete a self-evaluation. There is, by the way, no necessity to use the included evaluation. You may find numerous options over the Internet, or create your own. This latter option may be preferable because the evaluation will reflect the values and goals of your particular camp or retreat. Also, remember that the 360-degree process outlined here

Dear _____:

Leaders play a major part in any organization. Camp _____ has been under my leadership for the past _____ years. Unfortunately, leaders often do not have access to valuable information regarding their own job performance. While they may evaluate other staff members, leaders are often unaware of the evaluations that staff would like to give to them. Without feedback, improvement is hampered, if not made outright impossible.

I am asking that you complete the following evaluation on my leadership abilities. The entire evaluation will take no longer than 15 minutes. It can then be returned to me in the enclosed self-addressed stamped envelope. I am asking many peers and employees to complete this evaluation. The results will be collected and used to assist in my leadership development.

You will notice that there is no space for your name on the evaluation. These evaluations are anonymous. I will not know who completed each evaluation. This has been done so that participants will feel comfortable in giving honest feedback. Once again, the purpose of this evaluation is to assist in pinpointing my leadership deficits and strengths so that I can become a stronger leader for the camp.

Thank you for the assistance.

Sincerely,

is intended to foster the development of the leader. To use the 360-degree evaluation as an evaluation tool for all employees is a much more extensive project than outlined here. Many questions need to be answered prior to its introduction as the norm for an entire organization, including defining the purpose of the evaluation process, the culture of the organization, and the logistics of the evaluation.

Assessing the Results

When the evaluations start to come back, there might be a temptation to open them. WAIT! One evaluation by itself means nothing. A good one may evoke pleasant emotions in the leader. A bad evaluation may result in negative emotions. Don't put yourself through a possible roller coaster of emotional responses. When at least eighty percent have been returned (that means twelve evaluations if fifteen were mailed out or ten if twelve evaluations were mailed out), they can then be opened.

Don't overanalyze the results. If you have decided to implement this process alone, without the assistance of a supervisor or other support person, there may be a tendency for cognitive distortions to go unchecked. A bad evaluation is not the end of the world, nor does a positive one mean that you have no flaws. The results are not objective. These evaluations are merely the opinions of others.

The results are tallied as follows. The evaluations completed by the leader and his or her supervisor are kept separate from the others. The leader takes the returned evaluations from peers and employees and proceeds to average the responses characteristic by characteristic. This will not be difficult, though it might be tedious. So, for example, on the first specific characteristic on the evaluation, "Able to motivate those who work with him or her," a director has a total score of 38 in adding 11 responses from peers and employees. This score is then divided by the 11 responses for an average of 3.45. This is rounded down to 3. The leader then writes this down on the comparison sheet, shown on pages 177–180. His or her own response to this particular characteristic and the supervisor's responses are also listed. The leader does this same process for all 32 characteristics on the evaluation. Write down any particular comments from the evaluations that the leader finds valuable on the comparison sheet.

After the comparison sheet is completed for all of the characteristics, the leader can now compare his or her own responses to those of the others involved in the process. The job is to compare the accumulated feedback results from the participants to the leader's own self-evaluation. In which areas do the leader and participants agree? In what areas are there discrepancies between self and others' evaluations? The characteristics that show disagreement between self and others necessitate particular attention. If there is a discrepancy of two or more for a specific characteristic, this indicates that others have a different perspective of that particular skill. There may be some results that are confusing. Maybe the leader and supervisor mark one characteristic as strong while the evaluations of others indicate a weakness. There may not be one easy answer for this. Discuss the results with a supervisor or a person willing to assist in the process.

The leader may already know some of his or her weaknesses and therefore not find some of the results surprising. The leader always has the option to work on these. However, it is the responses that are different from that of the leader that truly deserve exploration. Based on this exploration, the leader can then decide what changes to make.

The level of anonymity can be increased by having an objective third party, such as one hired through a temporary employee business, tabulate average responses and transcribe all comments to one master feedback form. Such consolidation should not include the leader self-evaluation or that of the supervisor.

The leader can be assured that employees will also attempt to remain anonymous. For instance, your food service director may not add comments that include specifics of time or location that allow the comment to be attributed to him- or herself. On the one hand, the leader may feel hurt by such attempts to remain incognito. On the other hand, the leader may welcome the lack of detail because anonymity helps minimize the difference in power between supervisor and subordinate. By minimizing this power difference, the quality of the communication, as it pertains to an evaluation process, will be increased.

The leader can also welcome the details that reveal an employee's identity because they can be taken as an indication, or at least a test, of trust between leaders and direct reports. If direct reports did not trust the leader they would take whatever steps necessary to remain anonymous, including not participating in the process at all.

The Change Process

At this point, let's assume that either you have identified a change you wish to make in yourself or the input of others has indicated a need for some type of modification. If a leader can find no characteristic that needs improvement, that person is either truly extraordinary or is quite adept at fooling himself. This is cognitive distortion at its best! Every person, whether a leader or not, has some traits that complicate his or her life. In addition, every individual has some traits that complicate the lives of those with whom he or she interacts. A positive change may make their lives easier and less complicated.

Kilburg compiled a list of common desired changes for executives in business. All equally apply to the leader of a camp or retreat.

- Increase flexibility.
- Increase the capacity to manage an organization.
- Improve social competencies.
  - Increase social awareness.
  - Increase range of emotional responses.
  - Increase and maintain effective interpersonal relationships.
  - Decrease detrimental effects of negative emotions.
- Increase mental competencies.
  - Increase tolerance of ambiguity and randomness.
  - Improve stress management skills.
  - Improve capacity to learn and grow.
- Improve ability to manage career and advance professionally.
- Improve ability to manage tension between the organization, family, community, and personal needs (i.e., role conflict).
- Improve the effectiveness of the organization as a whole.

The process of identifying one's faults is a difficult and often intimidating one. You deserve some congratulations if, as you read the chapters on the components of the high-performance pyramid, you identified personal weaknesses in your leadership abilities. You deserve extra praise if you did indeed mail out an evaluation to employees, peers, and supervisor. Opening oneself to the feedback of others can be a frightening procedure. But don't make a mistake through thinking that the difficult work is behind you now. For while the process of diagnosing the problem areas is uncomfortable, the real challenge comes in change.

Change can be exceedingly difficult for individuals. Let me repeat that. Change can be very difficult. Many executive coaches spend long months, and sometimes years, attempting to galvanize successful change in their clients. Often they are successful. Other times, in spite of their best efforts, the coaching intervention is a failure or short-lived at best. As a familiar example, think of all the individuals, including yourself, who know the benefits of physical exercise but yet do not make it part of their daily lifestyle. Knowing that a problem exists or that a different approach would be more beneficial is far from enough to guarantee change. Argyris reminds us that "learning about these problems by listening to lectures, reading about them, or exploring them through cases is not adequate; an article or a book can pose some issues and get thinking started, but—in this area, at least—it cannot change behavior" (p. 82). He then goes on to detail a study of sixty top executives. All attended a week of lectures and discussion on leadership problems; the sessions were rated as of high quality, very useful, and truthful in their evaluation of leadership challenges. However, when these executives returned to their jobs, the vast majority were unable to make any changes in either themselves or their organizations. In another setting, three executives challenged Argyris on his prediction that they would be unable to change their behavior. They were confident that they could make desirable changes in themselves. They quickly recognized that they were unable to do so in spite of sincere and repeated efforts. Change can be very hard.

It is not only individuals that have a difficult time with change. Organizations also find it hard. In a study conducted by Nohria and Berkley and reported in the *Harvard Business Review*, the authors found that management interventions over the previous fifteen years rarely produced promised results. Every year or so a new management fad arrives on the scene and is taken up by a great number of organizations. Nohria and Berkley reported that in their interviews with managers from nearly a hundred different companies, seventy-five percent of them were disappointed with the results of the change. Even with the best of intentions, a change in an organization is more often than not far less successful than hoped for.

One of the major problems with implementing change on either an individual or an organizational level is a misconception regarding how change occurs. Change is not an either/or process in which an individual decides to make some type of modification and then proceeds to accomplish it or not. Perceived of in such simplistic terms, change is either something that happens or it doesn't. Psychologists have recognized the inherent difficulty in change and have studied the concept in order to attain superior results. Prochaska and DiClemente (1984) have led the way in both understanding and achieving change. These two authors have formulated the Transtheoretical Model of Change. Business people, therapists, medical professionals, and even sports professionals have utilized their findings.

The Transtheoretical Model of Change has three underlying beliefs.

1. A person is always in a state of change.
2. Change does not occur in an all-or-nothing fashion but rather through a series of stages.
3. Specific interventions to foster change are most appropriate at different stages.

In the first stage of change, precontemplation, the individual is either not aware that a change is necessary or believes that a desired change is impossible. For example, a woman may not have recognized that she has difficulty with the methods she uses to resolve problems until she read the chapter on mental capacity in this book. As another example, a man may have tried many diets only to gain the weight back. He therefore now believes that weight loss is impossible for himself. The best intervention for this early stage of change is an increase in awareness. New information or increased discomfort from resisting change may galvanize an individual to wonder if a change is necessary or really possible. Let's work with one example as a person goes through the stages of change.

Example

Theresa, a camp director, mailed out the evaluation on pages 173–176 to several employees and to the camp owner. She originally thought that the exercise would only serve to bolster her self-esteem, because she was fairly confident of her leadership abilities. She was quite distressed when the majority of evaluations from staff indicated a less flattering picture. One characteristic that was clear was that others did not believe that she gave enough appreciation for their hard work. They thought that she took them for granted.

In this example, Theresa had no awareness of the existing problem thus placing her in the precontemplation stage. New information made her suddenly aware that a problem might indeed exist.

In the second stage, contemplation, the individual recognizes that a problem exists and that a change might be beneficial. Recognition of a problem does not, of course, guarantee that the person will follow through on implementing a resolution. This is in large part due to the ambivalence associated with this stage. While there may be reasons for change, there are also competing reasons that a change would complicate the person's life. A person may recognize the need for more physical activity, but the time commitment will detract from an already too busy life. Sometimes a change requires just too much energy.

One of the recognized mistakes during the process of change is to spend too little time in the contemplation stage. The person involved recognizes a problem and immediately implements a solution. But like the man contemplating exercise, a sudden rush to join the gym will likely end in the expenditure of a large amount of money but little if any exercise after the first few weeks of membership. There may be very valid reasons why a change is not appropriate at this minute. In addition, the problem may be one the person can live with. Each person has to weigh both the advantages and disadvantages of implementing a change. This process should take some time.

Example

Theresa now realizes that she doesn't offer enough praise to her employees. She considers how much importance she wants to place on this particular problem. She had already decided to work on updating the camp programming, and she is collaborating with another camp director on a workshop for an upcoming conference. In addition, the counselor-in-training program needs some serious correction. She must consider whether she must pay immediate attention to her apparent indifference to staff. She has only so much time to devote to her job since she also has a family with its own issues to deal with.

Theresa recognizes the problem but is unsure whether she really wants to work on it due to other concerns she finds just as pressing. Each leader must decide whether a presenting problem deserves attention and effort. Not all problems need resolution. If the leader does decide to confront the problem, it is ideal if he or she takes the time necessary to evaluate all possible solutions and weigh the positive and negative effects of each. Through careful evaluation, the probable obstacles to each solution will become clearer thus narrowing down the range of options.

Preparation is the third stage of change. During this stage, the leader makes a commitment to change and begins a plan. The leader sets goals and takes preemptive steps to minimize interference from any obstacles that were considered in the contemplation stage.

Example

Theresa decides that the presenting problem is serious enough to warrant her attention. Her first thought had been to implement a bonus program offering cash rewards to all those staff members who remain the entire season. However, as she weighed the advantages and disadvantages of this solution, she recognized that it might be costly and might foster a mercenary reason to remain with the camp. This was not the best solution. After considering other options, she settles on something less costly but more valuable due to her already full schedule. She commits herself to engage in dialogue with each and every staff member at least once every week.

Recognize that after three stages in this theory of change, there has not yet been a single behavioral modification. These first three stages are the basic preparation for successful change. Theresa could well have spent weeks determining whether she was willing to invest in the change process. If she had decided to just change her behavior without adequate investigation in the contemplation and preparation stages, any attempted change would have been short lived. At a more personal level, if the reader has received some unexpected feedback in the evaluation, there is no need to actually change anything. People can learn to live with and compensate for huge personal leadership deficiencies without ever really addressing those deficiencies. As an example, visionary leaders are often advised to surround themselves with detail people, almost as if the two qualities were opposite and incompatible. (Don't be fooled by this example. Any visionary leader who is responsible for a sizable budget, a board report, or risk management is also competent with details. In small organizations, this is a necessity.) You should not attempt behavior change unless you are willing to explore potential solutions and complications. If you are unwilling, there is little hope that change will be successful. Consider how stubborn a resistance to change can be. Valuable relationships can be destroyed, integrity can be compromised, and organizational dysfunction can be exacerbated to the point of dissolving the business all because a leader resisted change. The computer giant IBM was nearly undone when executives laughed off Apple's insistence that everyone should have a computer on his or her desk. IBM held on so tightly to a mainframe model of computing that it nearly missed the personal computer revolution, which allowed Apple a short-lived competitive advantage.

The last two stages of the change process are where actual behaviors are altered. The fourth stage, the action stage, is where the individual begins to modify his or her behavior. This is also the most dangerous of the five stages. The individual has not yet reached stability with the new behavior. A bad mood, stress, or just too little time may result in a relapse in which the old, undesirable behavior reappears. Any interference can cause the person to decide to forgo any further attempt at the change. It is at this point that support, self-awareness, and management of obstacles are essential.

Example

Theresa attempts to spend five minutes with each staff member. For the first two weeks, she is quite successful and even begins to strongly believe that this investment of her time may well be worth it. Unfortunately, during the third week she becomes ill and spends almost two whole days in bed. She decides to not push herself to meet with each person but plans to begin again the next week. However, a valuable staff member suddenly quits and Theresa must quickly find a replacement. This search takes up much of her time during the fourth week. By the fifth week it is apparent that her goal of meeting with each staff member every week will not be successful.

Theresa could easily give up at this point. She may decide to drop the entire goal. She could formulate another solution for the presenting problem. She may even decide to continue with her planned goal because it was obviously resulting in more positive relationships with her staff members. Interference and problems are bound to occur no matter what solution a person decides upon. Many can be avoided with sufficient work in the earlier stages of contemplation and preparation. But even the most comprehensive plan cannot prepare for unexpected occurrences. Having the mental flexibility to deal with obstacles as well as the support of other people are often essential for getting through this stage.

Maintenance is the final stage. The individual's desired change has been accomplished, but there will always be the risk of a relapse of sorts. All of us have heard stories of individuals with drinking problems who stayed completely sober for years and then fell off the wagon. Everybody has the potential to revert to old behaviors. Long-term effort and revision of one's lifestyle have been found to be major factors in maintaining a change.

Example

Theresa has been talking to each staff member on a weekly basis for several months. There are, of course, weeks in which her motivation to continue this is less than others. In these weeks, she reminds herself of the benefits and forces herself to act (long-term effort). She also recognizes that there are certain weeks that are simply too filled with other activities, such as the first week of a new session, to permit this additional task. She therefore grants herself permission to miss these weeks. Instead, she accomplishes as much as she can of small but necessary tasks during that first week so that she can spend a little more time with staff the following week (lifestyle change).

The Reality of Change

While change can be very difficult some changes in behavior may seem to occur with little effort. Changes that occur over an extended period of time may be perceived as requiring little effort. For example, the young, frenetic program director intends to get more sleep on a regular basis, but he never seems to move in that direction. Twenty years later, that same person, now an executive director, may find himself organizing and prioritizing in such a way that he gets the sleep he needs on a regular basis. The perceived effort he put in to this change is mitigated by the long period over which this change actually became normal. Most likely the need for personal change and the response to that need has grown so gradually that sleeping more seems to be the natural thing to do. Similarly, obstacles to personal changes may have been minimized ever so slowly, and new, important skills have also developed ever so slowly. At any rate, changes that do occur, whether over a long or short period of time, can be explained and examined by this theory.

As stated earlier, one of the major obstacles to successful change is an incorrect assumption regarding change itself. It is rarely an all-or-nothing decision. One of the reasons that organizations and individuals fail to change is that change is approached without proper preparatory work. Significant change, the kind of change that makes major differences in personal impact, is a long-term process with repeated risks of relapse. To simply commit to a change without sufficient knowledge of the process almost guarantees failure.

Another important reason for the demonstrated inability to successfully implement change stems from homeostasis. As discussed earlier, individuals have a comfortable set point from which they approach the world. Any movement away from this comfort zone activates automatic responses, bringing the person back into an acceptable range. All changes share at least two characteristics, an emotional response and an expenditure of energy. A change can bring up numerous emotions in an individual, including anticipation, dread, anger, hope, elation, and relief. A change also requires spending energy. Humans, however, are notorious for limiting their own physical energy expenditure to as minimal as possible. The more energy required for a change, the more difficult it will be to maintain it. Our emotional set point and our tendency toward inertia maintain a homeostasis that is not conducive to change.

There are concrete steps that any leader in any organization can take that will result in positive leadership facilitation. In this book, we have examined research in the physical, emotional, cognitive, and spiritual realms. Most likely, you have identified some areas in which you are highly capable and other areas that need development. The evaluation method described in this chapter may also be able to give you some feedback about which areas other people see as requiring improvement. Perhaps there are only a few areas that really need some type of intervention thus making an improvement plan quite manageable. Other leaders may have found numerous performance obstacles and, as a result, are baffled how to begin the process. Fortunately, as a first step, there is a general strategy that has been found to positively affect leadership ability: Increase the credibility of the leader.

As reported by Conger, credibility grows out of two sources: expertise and relationships. "People are considered to have high levels of expertise if they have a history of sound judgment or have proven themselves knowledgeable and well informed…" (p. 232). Employees and peers would consider camp leaders experts if they have a thorough knowledge of their own camps and the camping industry as a whole. In addition, they should be able to demonstrate a comprehensive knowledge of leadership and management.

Regarding the second source of credibility, leaders who have demonstrated that they are empathic, are good listeners, and work in the best interests of other people have better relationships with employees. This raises the leader's credibility. There are some definite behaviors a leader can adopt that will increase relationship potential. The first is to expose oneself to evaluation. Asking how other people perceive the leader and how his or her behaviors interfere with their own job satisfaction is a critical step that allows others to begin to discuss their own weaknesses.

A second behavior is the recognition of the stress that employees and peers face and active attempts to reduce it. Leaders who act to reduce role conflict—for example, incompatible job responsibilities; overload, involving too many expectations and demands; job ambiguity, or unclear expectations about the work role; and conflict between work and family—will maintain better relationships (Griffeth and Hom).

A person who has read this book through, completed the accompanying work text, and implemented the 360-degree evaluation process is set to increase his or her credibility in the workplace. You now have a much more comprehensive understanding of the capacities and challenges that each leader must face, an expertise requirement. You have also allowed others to give honest feedback regarding leadership abilities, a relationship requirement. If the leader does decide, after a suitable time spent in contemplation and preparation, to change certain behaviors, this will augment his or her credibility. Remember though, that change is fraught with challenges and you are always at risk for relapse. A half-hearted attempt or one that fails may do damage to the leader's reputation. There is no doubt, though, that change is possible with the right support and planning. If you decide to change, go for it!

Summary of Key Points

1. Input from numerous sources is necessary for a comprehensive evaluation of a leader.

2. Change is not an either/or process in which an individual decides to make some type of modification and then proceeds to accomplish it or not. Change is actually a long-term process requiring ongoing effort.

3. Psychologists have broken down change into a five-stage process consisting of precontemplation, contemplation, preparation, action, and maintenance.

4. Due to the tendency toward homeostasis, humans resist change.

5. Leaders who are unsure where to begin the change process can focus on building their credibility through increasing their expertise and strengthening work relationships.

CHAPTER 8

COACHING AND TRAINING

Although ideas and suggestions about training could be a book in itself, it is important to at least briefly touch on the topic. Attendance at a training session does not guarantee a change in behavior, even though that is usually the intent of training: to change behavior. Consider how many conference sessions you have attended in your lifetime. How many gave you information that you made use of? How many can you actually recall? Simply requiring an individual to attend a training of some sort is no guarantee of success.

Research suggests that trainings without follow-up lead to poor results. For example, individuals who attend a five-day training on increasing computer skills will probably take some valuable material away to apply to their own jobs. This is particularly true if they have elected the training and are ready to learn. However, the majority of the material at a training session will not be applied because it is soon forgotten. This applies even to a five-day training session! Think of the success of a training that purports to teach skills in an hour or two. There will be very little.

What we do know is that training, when combined with practice of new skills *and* ongoing feedback, leads to far better and more consistent results. Your job as a director is not simply to give an hour-long training session on the topic of emotional management and then to hope that staff members walk away with something valuable. This almost guarantees failure. **Your job is to coach your supervisory staff to become better leaders. This requires the same protocol that you need for your own development: identify needs, educate staff on those needs, evaluate, and give feedback.** With this in mind, we can now discuss the optimal use of the trainings included in this book. The first step is a monthly or bimonthly training on a particular topic for supervisory staff in an informal setting. Here they will learn specific material that is necessary for their success as leaders. This is followed by individual supervision in which personal weaknesses and strengths are identified and discussed. The training ends with a series of questions that the director can address with staff members individually to better evaluate leadership capabilities. You can offer feedback regarding what you have seen in their performance that applies to the training topic(s).

Supervisors can also be asked to read this text and complete a copy of the workbook on their own. It would behoove directors to individually meet with each supervisory staff member each week to discuss not only the necessities of camp existence but also to track the attempts at leadership change he or she has put into place. Individual supervision is the place to discuss the success or lack of success in leadership and to receive feedback from the director. In my experience, too many individual supervisory sessions focus on the bureaucratic requirements of daily camp life and focus little attention on performance. This is often due to a lack of knowledge and experience on the part of the director. **Use supervisory sessions to develop the leadership skills of your staff.** These sessions are the appropriate place for feedback.

I have encountered several common concerns by directors regarding individual supervision. First, many say it takes too much time. The only response I can give is that there really is no other way for you to develop leaders. Supervisory sessions that include all supervisory staff are not often conducive to the change process. Change occurs within the confines of a trusting relationship. Even the director should seek assistance with personal change through a supportive, trusting relationship. Most groups do not offer the trust that a one-on-one relationship can foster.

Second, directors of seasonal camps that have supervisory staff in attendance for only two months often balk at such an intervention. My response to this is that such concerted efforts to develop a leader will likely equate with staff retention and return. This is for all staff, including supervisors and their direct reports. Since supervisors have the greatest influence on the satisfaction of other staff members, a good supervisor will net fewer resignations, fewer terminations, and a higher return rate. The harried seasonal camp director can always choose just one or two training topics to focus on for that season. Always keep in mind that the training is of far less importance than the individual supervision. One training accompanied by excellent individual supervision will be far more valuable than a mere series of training sessions without follow-up.

Finally, you can only assist staff members to grow if they trust you and feel safe in the relationship. If staff members do not trust you, these trainings and individual supervisory sessions will be of little value. If there is only one staff member who has an uncomfortable relationship with you, training sessions allow a perfect time to use your new leadership skills to gently approach the individual, ascertain the reason for the problem, and make plans to resolve it. On the other hand, if most of your staff members do not find you a safe person, it is time to do some serious work on yourself.

Feedback, such as with the evaluation concluding this book, will indicate how staff members perceive you.

In conclusion, there is no need to follow these trainings to the letter. The trainings are formulated so that you can match them to your own style. **Consider them outlines, not comprehensive presentations.** Some training manuals on the market tell you exactly what to say and do. The trainings in this text do not. Use the general outline as you see fit. I recommend, though, that you utilize the training on general leadership qualities first so as to lay a foundation for further work. Remember, training sessions are only the first and probably least important step in the process of leadership cultivation. Each training session is only a first opportunity for staff members to learn new material and consider its role in their leadership. The real work occurs in the individual supervision sessions and daily interactions with staff. For success, supervisory staff should be taught the material, be given a chance to evaluate themselves in regard to it, receive feedback from the director, and implement a change plan if needed. Readings from the text and workbook material can be used as supplements at any time. The director can consider the use of the evaluation tool concluding this text as a source of anonymous staff feedback.

General Leadership Training

Supplies Needed:

> Board or easel and paper
> Marker or chalk

1) Welcome members to the training.

2) Ask members to join with a partner. Each group is to discuss the best supervisor they have worked with.

3) Ask members to formulate a list of positive leadership qualities. *(Write on board or easel.)*

4) Have groups discuss the worst supervisor they have worked with.

5) Ask members to formulate a list of negative leadership qualities. *(Write on board or easel.)*

6) Ask members if they want to be remembered as a good supervisor or a bad supervisor by their staff. All will, of course, want to be remembered as a good supervisor. Ask why this is important to them.

7) Give reasons why this is important to you as the camp director. Some reasons are as follows.

a) More staff cohesion

b) Fewer problems to deal with

c) More time to focus on other issues

d) Less staff turnover

8) Describe some of the roles that the supervisory position entails. *(Write roles on board or easel.)*

a) Disturbance handler—coping with the problems of camp in order to assure its smooth functioning

  i) Have members list some disturbances they expect.

b) Entrepreneur—making positive and creative changes in the camp

  i) Have members discuss some positive changes they want to apply to camp.

c) Spokesperson—the role of presenting information to the camp director from the supervisor's direct staff

d) Disseminator—the role of passing information from the director to the direct staff

  i) Have members discuss some of the information that will have to pass from staff to director and from director to staff.

e) Monitor—watching what occurs in camp for problems and chances for positive growth

  i) Have members discuss some of the occurrences they should monitor, such as treatment of the campers.

f) Support—the role of supporting the growth of staff and being there as a support in difficult times

  i) Have members discuss what camp occurrences could require the support role (e.g., a staff member receives a phone call about a death in the family).

9) Ask members to discuss which of the roles they are most comfortable with and those they are uncomfortable with.

10) Explain that a staff member's direct supervisor is the most critical factor in an employee's job satisfaction.

11) Explain that there are few natural-born leaders. Most must be developed.

12) Explain the process of leadership development that this program will utilize.

   a) Training sessions will be designed to present information.

   b) Individual supervision sessions will focus on the needs that became evident in the trainings.

   c) Feedback will come from the director to discuss success or lack of success in the change process.

   d) Workbook and text (optional)

   e) 360-degree evaluation (optional)

13) Explain the schedule for individual supervision you will use.

14) Field questions.

Questions for Individual Supervision

1) Of the roles we discussed, which do you see as your strengths? Your weaknesses?

2) How well do you handle constructive feedback?

3) What do you think will be your greatest challenge as a supervisor?

4) What do you want to achieve as a supervisor?

5) What fears do you have as a supervisor?

Physical Capacity Training

Supplies Needed:

Board or easel
Chalk or markers

1) Ask the group to formulate a list of components necessary for a healthy lifestyle. *(Write on board or easel.)* Some common responses are as follows

   a) Sleep

   b) Fruits and vegetables

   c) Vacation

2) Present the four most essential components of a healthy lifestyle.

   a) Diet

    b) Physical activity

    c) Stress management

    d) Rest

3) Discuss which components from the lists under 1 and 2 are lacking in camp for staff.

4) Today's session will focus on the last three, specifically since the diet at camp is often beyond an individual's control.

5) Physical activity

    a) Explain that as you move higher into administrative positions, the more sedentary your responsibilities become.

    b) With a partner, discuss some of the ways members have become more sedentary.

    c) With a partner, discuss the responsibilities in your supervisory position that are not sedentary.

    d) As a group, discuss some methods to maintain physical activity in camp.

6) Stress management

    a) As a group, list stressors of camp life. *(Write on board or easel.)*

    b) Explain that stress can be either good or bad. Good stress challenges us, while bad stress overwhelms us.

    c) Explain that bad stress results in a decrease in the brain's ability to solve problems and be creative.

    d) List three methods of managing stress. *(Write on board or easel.)*

        i) Problem focused—an attempt to directly intervene with a problem or stressor

         • Present or ask for an example.

        ii) Social—the use of other people for support

         • Present or ask for an example.

        iii) Avoidance—avoiding the stressor as much as possible

         • Present (or ask for) an example.

    e) Explain that all methods of managing stress can be harmful or helpful depending on the given stressors. Give an example of a woman with chest pain who uses the avoidance method. Is this good or bad?

    f) Explain that staff will often use social and avoidance as their options for stress management.

g) As a group, discuss the advantages and disadvantages of relying on these two methods.

7) Rest

a) Explain that no research has definitely proved the reason for sleep. What is known is that a lack of sleep results in impaired health and in delayed mental functioning. A sustained sleep deficit can result in death.

b) As a group, discuss some camp occurrences that interfere with sleep.

c) As a group, brainstorm possible solutions for these occurrences.

8) As a group, list benefits of a healthy lifestyle. Some possible answers are as follows.

a) More energy

b) Better ability to manage stress

c) Better self-image

9) Answer concluding questions.

Questions for Individual Supervision

1) What are the worst stressors for you in camp?

2) How do you usually cope with stress? (Avoidance, social, etc.)

3) Do you want to become more physically active? If yes, how will this occur?

4) Out of the four major factors of a healthy lifestyle, which ones are you strongest with? Weakest with?

Emotional Capacity Training

Training #1: Recognition of Emotions

Supplies Needed:

Feelings list in Chapter 2 of the workbook
Board or easel and paper
Marker or chalk
Pens and paper

1) Ask participants about any knowledge they have regarding emotional intelligence.

2) Explain that emotional intelligence is probably the most important factor for successful leadership.

3) Explain that two of the most important emotional intelligence aspects for the workplace are as follows. *(Write on board or easel.)*

   a) Ability to recognize emotions

   b) Ability to manage emotions

4) Explain that this training is focused on recognition of emotions.

5) Hold an emotions competition in the following way. With a partner, write a list of as many emotions as possible in three minutes (director is timekeeper). At conclusion of three minutes, director asks each team for one emotion from their list and writes this on the board or easel. Any other team with that same emotion on their list can no longer use it. Continue until all emotions on lists have been presented. The team that has contributed the most emotions is the winner.

6) Explain that many individuals, especially men, tend to recognize only four emotions in themselves: anger, fear, sadness, and happiness.

7) With the same partner from step 5, each person chooses three emotions from the list and discusses experiences in life when these emotions occurred.

8) Hand out emotions list and peruse for any emotions missed in the contest.

9) Ask all staff members to list the advantages of having a more comprehensive vocabulary of emotions. Some probable answers will be as follows.

   a) Better ability to manage emotions when they are more recognizable

   b) More insight into what is going on inside oneself

   c) Better ability to recognize emotions in others

10) Explain that emotions exist for a reason and that they have been evident in humans from the earliest times. The three purposes of emotions are as follows.

   a) To give information to self

   b) To prepare a person for action

   c) To give information to other individuals

11) Tell the story of a man walking through the forest and encountering a bear from Chapter 4. How does the emotion of fear help this man? What would happen if he did not experience fear? (He might continue to approach it and be attacked.)

12) Explain that, in general, supervisors are much less aware of the emotions of their staff than the staff is of the supervisor's emotions. Staff members monitor supervisors for emotions so they know how to respond to him or her. This does not often happen in the reverse order.

13) Ask members if they can recall a time that they could tell from your behavior that you, the camp director, were mad even though you never actually told them.

14) Explain that successful leaders recognize emotions not only in themselves but also in others.

15) Discuss with a partner three times that emotions were encountered with another staff member.

16) As a large group discuss some of the challenges of dealing with staff emotional displays.

17) Ask staff members to consider the following question before their next individual supervision: "Would your staff members say that you are good at recognizing their emotions?"

18) Answer final questions.

Questions for Individual Supervision

1) Are you good at recognizing emotions occurring in yourself?
2) Are you good at recognizing emotions in your staff?
3) When do your emotions interfere with your job as a supervisor?

Training #2: Management of Personal Emotions

Note: this is a longer training and may require ninety minutes. You can split it into two sessions if necessary.

Supplies Needed:

Board or easel and paper
Marker or chalk

1) Reiterate the role of emotional intelligence as one of the most important factors in leadership success.

2) Reiterate two of the most important emotional intelligence aspects for the workplace *(Write on board or easel.)*

   a) Ability to recognize emotions

   b) Ability to manage emotions

3) Explain that this training will focus on the second of the abilities— emotional management.

4) Ask how many believe they can hide their emotions from staff. If, for example, you are experiencing sadness, is it easy to hide it from subordinates?

5) With a partner, try the following experiment.

   a) Tell your partner a funny story or incident.

   b) Allow a few minutes for partners to share their story.

   c) Afterwards, each attempts to fake a smile.

   d) Partner should try to identify the difference between the natural smile and the smile that was forced.

   e) As a large group, ask what were the noticeable differences between the fake smile and the natural one.

   f) As a large group, ask what was easier, a natural smile or a forced one.

   g) Explain that faking emotions is very difficult and that staff can often see through the act.

6) Describe emotional leakage in which the supervisor's emotions will inadvertently leak out and affect other staff members, particularly those that report directly to the supervisor. Remind supervisors that their staff is acutely aware of the emotions of their boss.

7) Ask members if they recall the three purposes of emotions.

   a) Give information to self.

   b) Prepare a person for action.

   c) Give information to other individuals.

8) With a partner, have each member discuss an incident of intense emotion that occurred in the workplace or at home, if necessary. Have them explain how it affected their ability to perform their job.

9) Present methods to deal with emotions.

a) Inform staff that there are only three known ways to change an emotion almost immediately: sex, drugs use, and food. Unfortunately the first two are not acceptable camp behaviors and the third is not under their control unless dining hall supervisory staff is present.

b) Another method is to just wait the emotion out, since all intense emotions dissipate quickly and leave an easier to manage "bad mood" that may last for days.

c) A third method of coping with intense emotion is expressing the emotions to the individual(s) who initiated the situation. Most negative emotions that happen in camp will occur in our interactions with other people. Have students perform the following activity.

i) With a partner, discuss a time that expression of emotion worked.

ii) With a partner, discuss a time that expression did not work so well.

iii) As a group, discuss obstacles to expressing negative emotion to another person. Some common responses are as follows.

- Self-doubt
- Fear of consequences
- Fear of loss of self-control

10) Present the guidelines for successful expression. *(Write on board or easel.)*

a) Describe the emotion.

b) Describe the behavior that led to the emotion.

c) Take responsibility for your own role in the problem.

d) Check assumptions.

e) Show a commitment to the relationship.

11) Have two volunteers role play the following scenario using the guidelines in step 10. "Pat had already reprimanded Chris for returning late from his evening off just last week. Tonight Chris returns home more than an hour after curfew from a trip to town. Pat, the supervisor, is furious."

a) An example of an appropriate response is: "Chris, I'm feeling very angry right now (a). This is the second time you've returned late in a week, and we've already discussed this problem (b). Maybe I wasn't clear in what I needed you to do (c). I can't help but think that you are doing this on purpose and that you couldn't care less about the rules (d). I want us to work together well (e)."

12) Explain that the tone of voice should be calm and respectful.

13) Have staff members come up with a common supervisor/employee problem in your camp. Have members partner and role play the example using the guidelines.

14) Discuss advantages and disadvantages of using the guidelines for expressing emotions.

15) Discuss any obstacles that may occur in use of these guidelines.

16) Address any final questions.

Questions for Individual Supervision

1) "Do you express your emotions responsibly?"

2) "How do your emotions affect your leadership performance?"

3) Role play an expression of emotions.

4) "Do you feel that you could express your emotions to me (as the director)?"

5) "Is the five-step process for expression of emotions something that you would like to make use of? Why or why not? If yes, how do you plan on implementing it?

Training #3: Management of Staff Emotions

Supplies Needed:

Board or easel and paper
Marker or chalk

1) Explain that so far we have worked on recognition of our own emotions and those of the staff we supervise. We have also looked at methods to productively express our emotions. Now we will look at methods of coping with the emotional displays of staff.

2) Brainstorm some of the stressors that the staff we supervise encounter in their jobs.

3) Have each member share an incident of staff member anger with a partner.

COACHING AND TRAINING-155

4) Ask members how we respond when another person expresses their anger to us. Some of the common responses are as follows.

   a) Resentment

   b) Our own anger builds

   c) Fear

5) Explain that most staff will not directly confront a leader. Instead, they talk among themselves. This does not solve the present problem and only provokes emotions in other staff.

6) Our job as supervisors is to assist staff members to express their emotions to us in a productive way.

7) Reiterate guidelines for expression of emotions. *(Write on board or easel.)*

   a) Describe the emotion.

   b) Describe the behavior that led to the emotion.

   c) Take responsibility for own role in the problem.

   d) Check assumptions.

   e) Show a commitment to the relationship.

8) Have two volunteers role play the following scenario using the above guidelines: "A counselor is furious because his supervisor has to move him to another unit due to a staff shortage. This staff member was happy in his unit." Supervisor is to assist the member to express the emotion in an appropriate fashion. For example, the supervisor could ask the following questions.

   a) It sounds like you're really angry.

   b) I really want to understand your anger. Could you give me the exact reason for it?

   c) I had to switch you to another unit due to a staff shortage.

   d) Why do you think I picked you?

   e) I want you to be able to continue to do a good job, and I enjoy our working relationship together. I'll help you in any way possible during this transition.

9) Get feedback from all participants during the process of the role play.

10) Staff will not feel free to come to us to express emotions unless they feel the relationship is safe.

11) Ask members how they would define a safe relationship.

12) A safe relationship is one in which a person can express his or her emotions without fear of retribution and in which the other person will truly listen though not necessarily agree.

13) Explain that relationships can be judged for safety by their communication styles.

14) Describe the four levels of communication. *(Write on board or easel.)*

   a) Niceties—An individual presents only pleasantries (e.g., "Good afternoon.").

   b) Factual information—An individual presents information of a factual nature (e.g., "I need that list by tonight at five o'clock.").

   c) Thoughts and ideas—An individual presents information about internal ideas, plans, or thoughts. This remains on a cognitive level.

   d) Emotions—An individual presents information about his or her emotions.

15) Explain that our relationships with staff may involve all of these levels. However, those individuals who are willing to share thoughts and particularly emotions are really opening up to us. This indicates a trust in the relationship.

16) Have members discuss some examples of the levels of communication they experience with different camp staff.

17) Ask members to consider which level they are at with their direct subordinates. The higher the level, the more safe the relationship is.

18) Address final questions.

Questions for Individual Supervision

1) How do you typically manage staff members' emotional displays?

2) What is your usual communication level with your direct staff?

3) Do you create a safe relationship with your direct staff?

4) What would it take to create a safe relationship with your staff?

5) What are the obstacles to creating a safe relationship with your staff?

Training #4: Anger

Supplies Needed:

Board or easel and paper
Marker or chalk

1) Explain that we have already discussed recognition and management of emotions in our staff and in ourselves. Anger, however, requires its own session. Anger will probably be the most common negative emotion we will encounter in our staff.

2) Explain that there are both productive and nonproductive ways to deal with the emotion of anger.

3) Have members brainstorm productive ways to handle anger. *(Write on board or easel.)* Some common responses include the following.

 a) Talking to the source of the anger (expression)

 b) Waiting until the anger passes

 c) Exercise

4) Have members brainstorm nonproductive ways to handle anger. *(Write on board or easel.)* Some common responses include the following.

 a) Revenge

 b) Silent treatment

 c) Lackluster performance

5) Explain that anger is a sign that something is wrong. Many supervisors respond to an angry staff member by becoming angry themselves. The first and most important step is to prevent oneself from becoming angry.

6) Ask group members if they know what happens inside their brain when they become angry? *(Accept several answers.)* Give the following explanation.

 Anger results in an immediate fight or flight reaction. An angry individual has limited ability to problem solve or think clearly. This applies equally to supervisors and staff.

7) In order to communicate effectively with an angry staff member, we need to move into upper levels of communication, including discussion of thoughts and emotions.

8) Remind staff that unless a safe relationship has developed between the two parties, discussions at these levels will be difficult.

9) Anger education

 a) Explain that many people perceive as anger as in Figure 8.1.

(Draw Figure 8.1 on board or easel.)

Figure 8.1 An event triggers anger.

b) Have members give several examples.

Explain that anger is actually a secondary emotion as in Figure 8.2. *(Draw Figure 8.2 on board or easel.)*

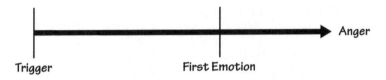

Figure 8.2 Anger is a secondary emotion.

c) Give the following example to members. "Carla's unit had to be dismissed early from the dining hall due to their behavior. Later the camp director says to Carla, 'If you can't do your job, I'll find somebody else.'" Name some emotions Carla might experience other than anger. Some probable responses are as follows.

i) Fear

ii) Hurt

iii) Insulted

d) Explain that the first emotion in the anger illustration is usually one of powerlessness. This includes guilt, fear, shame, and embarrassment. Such emotions may lead to vulnerability. The brain automatically changes such emotions into anger, an emotion of power and self-protection.

e) Read the following story and ask members to use the anger illustration from step c and to decide on the trigger and the possible first emotions for Arthur. "Arthur and Diane are two counselors who are in the beginning stages of a romantic relationship. Diane has a very bad morning with some of the girls in her bunk. At lunch, Arthur attempts to speak to Diane, but she appears to lack interest. Arthur storms off in a fury, exclaiming 'Women never know what they want!' "

f) Reiterate that when we encounter an angry staff member we are actually seeing one who is responding to hurt or one who is not feeling safe.

g) Explain that there is one more important aspect to anger that should be addressed: the role of thoughts.

(Draw Figure 8.3 on the board or easel.)

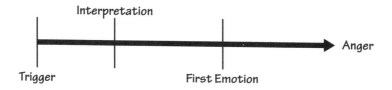

Figure 8.3 The brain interprets an event quickly.

h) Explain that the brain works very quickly and that when we encounter a trigger we will interpret it in a matter of seconds or less.

i) Use the example from step f. Ask the following questions. What were some of the immediate thoughts that entered Arthur's mind when Diane appeared to be acting distant toward him? *(Accept several answers.)*

Some possible answers are as follows.

i) "She doesn't like me anymore."

ii) "She cares more about her campers than she does about me."

j) Explain that an angry staff member has interpreted an action as threatening or hurtful. This interpretation could be right or it could be wrong.

k) Ask members if they have ever been angry and then found out they were wrong (i.e., if they have interpreted a trigger in a wrong way). Ask for an example or two.

l) Explain that when dealing with an angry staff member, it is important to ask what they think happened (i.e., how they interpret the anger-provoking trigger).

m)In conclusion, dealing with an angry staff member requires dis-

cussing his or her interpretations and first emotions in addition
to the five guidelines for expression of emotion discussed in the
last two trainings.

n) Explain that a supervisor's safety is paramount. Do not attempt
to meet with a staff member if you believe that there could be
personal danger to you.

Questions for Individual Supervision

1) Is your own anger management a problem?
2) Can you tolerate staff anger?
3) What do you need to work on in regard to anger for yourself or
your staff?

Mental Capacity Training

*Note: Mental capacity trainings are usually very informative for staff. They
may have attended years of schooling, but rarely have they been taught
how to think more productively. This most often occurs within the confines of therapy.*

Training #1: Distorted Thinking

Supplies Needed:

Board or easel and paper
Marker or chalk
Copy of illusion in Chapter 8 of the workbook for each member
Paper and pens

1) Explain that today we will discuss an obstacle to successful leadership: reliance on one's own judgments in making decisions.
2) Hand out a copy of the illusion to each staff member **face down** so
that they cannot see the picture. Tell them that you will give them
exactly four seconds to turn over the picture and look at it. At the
end of four seconds turn the papers face down again. No one should
discuss what he or she saw. Collect the papers. Now give a slip of
paper and pen to each participant. They are to silently write what
they saw in the picture. Each member then tells what he or she
wrote as a description.

There will likely be different answers. If everybody saw the same picture, this is just as workable also.

Hand out the illusion again and explain that it can be either a rabbit or a duck.

3) Explain that the human brain developed to prize speed over accuracy. A quick decision often resulted in survival. An ancestor who witnessed a large, black animal coming at him but who decided to wait until he was certain what it was most likely did not live long enough to pass on his genetic codes. A less accurate decision could also result in death but had far more chances of correction from the input of others.

4) Explain that the human brain has not changed much from that of our ancestors. We too make very quick decisions without a determination of accuracy. Often what we encounter is ambiguous and can be interpreted in numerous ways, such as the illusion.

5) With a partner, have each member discusses a time he or she made a quick decision that turned out to be wrong.

6) Discuss automatic thoughts using the following steps.

   a) Explain that when we encounter an ambiguous stimulus, our first interpretation can be wrong.

   b) Present the following scenario. "You are doing cabin inspections. Two counselors are unaware that you are outside their cabin.

You hear your name and then uproarious laughter. What would be the first thoughts that occur to you?"

Some possible responses are as follows.

i) They're making fun of me.

ii) So that's what they think of me!

iii) I'll get you back, you @#$%^&*!!!!

c) Ask if there any other possible interpretations for this occurrence.

7) Explain that poor leaders will act upon their first thoughts. These first thoughts are called automatic thoughts because they occur automatically. You do not will them to appear.

a) Ask members for suggestions on how to cope with automatic thoughts.

b) Explain that we must learn to slow down and to think before acting, which is just the opposite of how our brain works. Remember that our first thoughts are often wrong.

c) Present the following scenario. "You come into my office (the office of the camp director). I look up from my desk with an angry face and tell you to come back later. What are the first thoughts that occur in your head?"

Discuss several answers.

d) Ask for several possible reasons for the director's behavior.

e) Explain that the director presented ambiguous behavior that could lead to several interpretations.

f) Ask for several methods to deal with this situation.

8) Remind supervisors that their staff will also experience automatic thoughts when they encounter ambiguous behavior.

9) With a partner, have each member discuss a time that a staff member misinterpreted his or her behavior.

10) Address final questions.

Questions for Individual Supervision

1) Would your direct staff say that you often misinterpret their behavior?

2) Discuss a recent incident with a problematic employee. What were your automatic thoughts after the incident?

3) Do you think that you jump to conclusions too often?

Training #2: Distorted Thinking (Continued)

Supplies Needed:

Board or easel and paper
Marker or chalk

1) Ask members to explain the concept of speed versus accuracy in relation to the brain.

2) Ask members to explain the concept of automatic thoughts.

3) Ask each member to think of a time since the last session in which he or she noticed the influence of automatic thoughts in their supervisory duties. Ask each member to share this with the group.

4) Explain that for this session, we are going to take an advanced look at automatic thoughts. Psychological research has determined that automatic thoughts can be classified into categories.

5) Write labels on board or easel.

a) Exaggeration—The importance of an event is greatly exaggerated.

  i) Give examples.

   • Positive exaggeration: Charles makes eye contact with LeDawn. She smiles. The first thought that occurs in his head is, "she really likes me."

   • Negative exaggeration: Charles is called to the camp director's office. His first interpretation is, "I'm about to get fired."

  ii) Explain that these interpretations could be right but they could also be wrong.

  iii) Ask for examples of exaggeration that individuals have seen in the workplace.

b) Minimization—The effects of a potentially serious event are underestimated.

  i) Give the following example. "Rudy has been asked to come over to the girls' side of camp after curfew. This is a direct violation of camp policy. His thoughts are, 'What's the big deal?' and 'I won't get caught anyway.' "

  ii) Explain that minimization often results in risk-taking behaviors.

  iii) Ask for examples of minimization that individuals have seen in the workplace.

c) Personalization—An event is interpreted as a personal attack.

 i) Offer the following examples.

 • Positive personalization: Dee sees another staff member attempting to sneak a cake and balloons into the camp office. Her first thought is, "They must be planning a party for me for all the good work I'm doing."

 • Negative personalization: Dee hears her name mentioned by some campers in passing. This is followed by laughter. Her first thought is, "They're making fun of me."

 ii) Ask for examples of personalization that individuals have seen in the workplace.

6) Explain that these are only three types from a long list of automatic thought categories. **They will occur in camp.**

7) Explain that each individual uses certain automatic thought types more than others. One individual may tend to use personalization often, while another rarely ever does. This second person, however, tends to use exaggeration fairly often.

8) Ask each staff member to describe the distortions that are most common for him or her.

9) Explain that the most successful method for dealing with automatic thoughts is recognition and disputation.

 a) A person must first recognize the thoughts as they occur. This is a skill that can be learned but is not one that most people have acquired. Continual "catching" of one's thoughts as they are occurring is essential. We will discuss the problems that members' automatic thoughts are causing for yourself and your staff.

 b) Disputation involves questioning your automatic thoughts. Are your first thoughts accurate? Some good questions to ask after recognition of automatic thoughts follow.

 i) Is there another possible explanation for this event other than my first interpretation?

 ii) How important is this event to me? Is it worth my time and effort?

 c) Have members recall some of the examples of exaggeration, minimization, and personalization from above. Have them take turns verbalizing the automatic thoughts and then use disputation to counter them. The following are examples.

     i) Automatic thought: They're laughing at me!

     ii) Disputation: They could be laughing at me, but there could be another explanation.

     iii) Automatic thought: I won't get caught.

     iv) Disputation: I might get caught. Am I willing to accept the repercussions?

10) Explain that recognition and disputation skills really can influence the way you react to occurrences in camp in a positive way.

11) Address final questions.

Questions for Individual Supervision

1) How have personalization, exaggeration, and minimization affected your supervisory performance?

2) You stated in the training that _____ was the most common automatic thought type for you. Since the training, have you attempted to be more conscious of this? Explain an incident in which this occurred.

3) How do you plan on modifying this tendency toward an automatic thought pattern?

Note: It is beneficial to have staff members discuss their automatic thoughts and practice disputation skills regarding occurrences in camp and interactions with staff during individual supervision. Directors might consider spending several minutes each session to check in and practice recognition and disputation skills.

Training #3: Selective Attention

Supplies Needed:

Board or easel and paper
Marker or chalk
Paper and pens
Copies of "busy picture" and related questions from Chapter 8 in the workbook

1) Hand out a copy of the busy picture to each staff member **face down** so that he or she cannot see the picture. Tell them that you

will give them exactly one minute to turn over the picture and look at it. At the end of one minute turn the papers **face down** again. No one should discuss what he or she saw. Collect the papers. Now give out a copy of the questions to each staff member face down. You will find the related questions in Chapter 8 of the workbook. Tell them that you will give them exactly four minutes to answer the questions. Each individual should work independently. At the end of four minutes, work must stop.

2) Have each person work with a partner. Have the partners compare answers to see how many they agree or disagree on. Allow several minutes for this as most teams will become very involved in this process.

3) Hand out the busy picture again and allow several minutes for teams to check their answers against the picture.

4) Explain that everybody in the room saw the exact same picture for the exact same period of time. Therefore we should have perfect agreement in answers.

5) Ask members of each team how many answers they shared that were wrong and right. (Note: I have yet to encounter a team that has had all the same answers—both right and wrong.)

6) Ask how this could happen since we all saw the same picture for the same amount of time. Why don't we all have the same answers?

   Allow several responses.

7) Explain that we are bombarded by sensations every second of our lives, both externally by sights, sounds, and smells and internally by pain, headaches, the sensation of our feet in our shoes, or the sensation of our back against the chair. Our brain can only handle one thing at a time, otherwise we become overwhelmed. Our brain deals with so many external and internal sensations by focusing our attention only on what is most important.

8) Give the example that if you were driving down the highway looking for a hotel, you would not likely attend to the restaurants that you passed. Likewise, if you were hungry, you would notice the restaurants, not the hotels.

9) Explain that much of what we perceive is based on the following two factors. *(Write on board or easel.)*

   a) Novelty—If an alligator walked through the dining hall, everybody would see it!

   b) What is important to us—A birdwatcher would see numerous birds on a nature walk while a nonbirdwatcher would see far fewer.

10) Have members discuss a time that they saw something that another person did not or that was described differently by two viewers.

11) Explain that because we are selective in our attention, we make decisions, sometimes important ones, based on limited information.

12) Explain that one method to circumvent this is to seek the input of others. However, staff may not give honest information to the boss.

13) Brainstorm several reasons why staff refrain from giving feedback to supervisors. (Fear, or they think the supervisor lacks interest.)

14) Ask staff to brainstorm some methods to deal with this dilemma. How do we get honest and important information from staff to make decisions?

15) Remind supervisors that the reason for this training is to increase leadership ability so that staff will think it is safe to give critical feedback.

16) In conclusion, remind staff that our own decisions are often faulty due to our limited perception abilities. We need to involve others in the process of making decisions since they may have information we need but cannot see.

17) Address final questions.

Questions for Individual Supervision

1) Who assists you in making decisions? Do you rely only on yourself?

2) What are the personal advantages of involving more people in the process?

3) What are the disadvantages of involving more people in the process?

4) Do you want to change the way you make decisions? Why or why not?

5) How often do staff members approach you with feedback on your performance?

Integrative Capacity Training

Training #1: Optimism

Supplies Needed:

Board or easel and paper
Marker or chalk

1) Explain that it is only in the recent past that researchers in the fields of psychology and medicine have begun to examine what is right with people instead of what is wrong. One goal of this new research

is to make people stronger and more productive, and to allow the activation of their potential.

2) As a group, have members list components of a satisfied life. *(Write on board or easel.)*

3) Explain that research has found several factors that influence satisfaction with life such as the following.

   a) A sense of hope

   b) Relationships

   c) Faith

   d) Motivation

4) Explain that today we will examine optimism, one specific component that you can begin working on immediately.

   a) Ask members to define optimism.

   b) Explain that optimism is experienced as positive expectations about the future.

   c) Explain that pessimistic individuals explain negative occurrences as follows.

      i) Permanent—It's going to last forever.

      ii) Personal—It's my fault.

      iii) Pervasive (affecting all areas of life)—Everything's ruined now.

5) Read the following vignette. "Aaron was on duty for his group of campers one evening while his co-counselors were in town. He heard several of the campers in one cabin laughing. Aaron stood outside the window and told them to go to sleep. This happened on several occasions over the next hour. It was only the next morning that it was discovered that the group of campers had joined together to cover another sleeping child in the cabin with shaving cream, deodorant, and toothpaste."

   a) Ask members to think of some pessimistic pervasive thoughts that might occur, such as, "I'm going to get fired now. This is the last time they'll let me work at this camp."

   b) Ask members to think of some pessimistic permanent thoughts that might occur, such as, "I'll never be able to work with kids."

   c) Ask members to think of some pessimistic personal thoughts that might occur, such as, "I'm such an idiot. I should have known better."

d) Explain that optimistic individuals explain negative occurrences in a different way. *(Write labels on board or easel.)*

   i) Temporary

   ii) External—The individual does not personally accept blame unless he is really responsible.

   iii) Circumscribed—The negative event affects some aspects of life, but not all aspects.

e) Read Aaron's vignette above again and ask for optimistic thoughts.

   Some responses are as follows.

   i) "I screwed up. I should have gone into the cabin and checked when I heard their laughing. I won't let that happen again." (Temporary thought)

   ii) "I told the director that we shouldn't place Michael and Donald in the same cabin." (External thought)

   iii) "Hopefully the fact that I do such a great job at the talent show will stop the director from getting too angry." (Circumscribed thought)

f) Individuals have a tendency to be either optimistic or pessimistic. Optimism can be learned through disputing the first thoughts that occur in our heads. This is similar to checking the validity of our automatic thoughts, which we covered in an earlier session. Our staff will also have a tendency toward optimism or pessimism.

g) Explain that optimistic supervisors tend to live more satisfied lives. This also positively affects relationships with their staff. However, even optimism must be tempered. Too much optimism may be interpreted as unrealistic.

6) Ask members to think of and share a personal experience with either pessimistic or optimistic thoughts.

7) Address final questions.

Questions for Individual Supervision

1) Are you an optimist or a pessimist?

2) How has your optimism or pessimism affected your relationship with your staff?

3) Have you become aware that any of your staff members are optimists or pessimists? What is it like to work with them?

Training #2: Motivation

Supplies Needed:

Board or easel and paper
Marker or chalk

1) Ask members to recall some of the factors that lead to a satisfied life, such as hope, optimism, and so on.
2) Explain that today we will discuss motivation.
3) Ask members for a definition of motivation.
4) Research has broken motivation down into two different types. *(Write on board or easel.)*
   a) Extrinsic—We do something in order to gain a particular goal or reward. For example, we work in order to get a paycheck. We go to school for a diploma.
   b) Intrinsic—We participate in an activity for the pure challenge or enjoyment of it, and no reward is necessary.
5) Ask members to list some of the tasks they perform at camp because it is their job, not because they enjoy performing them (e.g., cabin inspections, paperwork). These are examples of extrinsically motivating duties.
6) Ask members to list some of the activities they perform at camp because they enjoy doing them (e.g., acting, storytelling, sports). These are examples of intrinsically motivating duties.
7) Ask members to list some of the responsibilities that their staff perform that are extrinsically motivated.
8) Explain that our staff will need no assistance in completing intrinsically motivated tasks. On the other hand, for the extrinsically motivated activities, they may need our support and direction.
9) Ask members to brainstorm methods to motivate staff. *(Write on board or easel.)*
   a) Explain that there have been several proven methods to increase a person's motivation for a task. Though an individual may never become intrinsically motivated to perform it, he or she will need less extrinsic motivation. Some methods are as follows.
      i) Autonomy—This method allows the individual some choice in how to complete the task. To demonstrate this, have mem-

bers work in pairs to discuss one problem they have with staff members in regard to completing a task. How could you allow more autonomy with the task?

    ii) Competence—This method involves the skills and ability to complete a task. Demonstrate this method by having pairs of members discuss one problem they have with staff members in regard to completing a task. How could you make the staff more competent with the task?

10) Read the following vignette and brainstorm answers. "Pat is taking his unit on an overnight camping trip. He is well aware that his staff hates this activity and will do a minimal amount of work. They have no intrinsic motivation for this task. Usually Pat spends the entire night watching the staff as carefully as he watches the campers. He must give specific instructions and be very demanding on these overnight trips. How could he build more autonomy and competence into the trip so as to decrease the extrinsic motivation?"

11) Address final questions.

Questions for Individual Supervision

1) What are the tasks you perform that you need to force yourself to complete?

2) How could we build competence and autonomy into them?

3) What are the duties that you love to perform?

4) What motivation problems are you running into with your staff? How are you attempting to cope with them?

Performance Evaluation

This evaluation has been formulated to provide a camp director with the perspectives of many different individuals, including employees, peers, and supervisors.

Once the confidential responses have been tabulated, the results will be used to pinpoint the strengths and weaknesses of the leader and to design a plan for personal development. The purpose of this evaluation is for leaders to gain a better understanding of their leadership skills.

Please be honest in completing the form. There are two types of questions included. The first asks you to rank a specific characteristic of leadership as seen in this individual on a scale ranging from Never to Always. If a particular characteristic does not apply, there is also a space to mark Not Applicable. Circle the number that you believe most accurately applies.

0 .... Not Applicable
1 .... Never
2 .... Rarely
3 .... Sometimes
4 .... Often
5 .... Always

The second type of question asks for any comments you may have regarding specific characteristics. These spaces can be used for any specific information you think that the leader should know regarding his or her abilities and skills.

Leadership

	Not Applicable	Never	Rarely	Sometimes	Often	Always
Able to motivate those who work with him or her	0	1	2	3	4	5
Promotes a positive attitude in the workplace	0	1	2	3	4	5
Resolves team conflicts fairly	0	1	2	3	4	5
Utilizes the talents of staff to the best advantage	0	1	2	3	4	5
Promotes an atmosphere of teamwork and cooperation	0	1	2	3	4	5

Comments regarding leadership skills:

_____

_____

_____

Management

	Not Applicable	Never	Rarely	Sometimes	Often	Always
Delegates responsibility	0	1	2	3	4	5
Holds individuals accountable	0	1	2	3	4	5
Rewards achievement	0	1	2	3	4	5
Allocates resources fairly and for their best use	0	1	2	3	4	5
Uses clear criteria for job and performance evaluations	0	1	2	3	4	5

Comments regarding management skills:

_____

_____

_____

Interpersonal Skills

	Not Applicable	Never	Rarely	Sometimes	Often	Always
Is considerate of the emotions of others	0	1	2	3	4	5
Demonstrates the ability to manage his or her own emotions	0	1	2	3	4	5
Exhibits respect for others	0	1	2	3	4	5
Coaches and mentors others for their own development	0	1	2	3	4	5
Is approachable and easy to talk to	0	1	2	3	4	5

Comments regarding interpersonal skills:

_____

_____

_____

Communication Skills

	Not Applicable	Never	Rarely	Sometimes	Often	Always
Listens to the opinions of others	0	1	2	3	4	5
Actively seeks the opinions of others	0	1	2	3	4	5
Communicates in an effective manner	0	1	2	3	4	5
Gives honest and constructive feedback	0	1	2	3	4	5

Comments regarding communication skills:

_____

_____

_____

Judgment / Problem Solving

	Not Applicable	Never	Rarely	Sometimes	Often	Always
Thinks ahead and develops clear plans	0	1	2	3	4	5
Makes sound decisions when under pressure	0	1	2	3	4	5
Attempts to thoroughly assess a problem before taking action	0	1	2	3	4	5
Is creative in solving problems	0	1	2	3	4	5

Comments regarding judgment/problem solving skills:

_____

_____

_____

Knowledge

	Not Applicable	Never	Rarely	Sometimes	Often	Always
Exhibits knowledge of his or her particular field	0	1	2	3	4	5
Shares that knowledge with others	0	1	2	3	4	5

Keeps informed of new material and changes in the field	0	1	2	3	4	5

Comments regarding knowledge skills:

_____

_____

_____

Personal Characteristics

	Not Applicable	Never	Rarely	Sometimes	Often	Always
Is organized	0	1	2	3	4	5
Has a good work ethic	0	1	2	3	4	5
Demonstrates responsibility on the job	0	1	2	3	4	5
Maintains a high energy level	0	1	2	3	4	5
Admits to mistakes	0	1	2	3	4	5
Accepts criticism	0	1	2	3	4	5

Comments regarding personal characteristics skills:

_____

_____

_____

Comparison Sheet

Instructions:

1. Average the combined score for peers and employees for each characteristic and place score into the corresponding box.
2. If a supervisor completed the evaluation, place the score for each characteristic into the appropriate box.
3. Place your own score for each characteristic into the appropriate box.
4. Any characteristic exhibiting a difference of two or more points among any of the boxes needs exploration.

Characteristic	Average of peers and employees	Supervisor	Self
1. Able to motivate those who work with him or her			
2. Promotes a positive attitude in the workplace			
3. Resolves team conflicts fairly			
4. Utilizes the talents of staff to the best advantage			
5. Promotes an atmosphere of teamwork and cooperation			
6. Delegates responsibility			
7. Holds individuals accountable			
8. Rewards achievement			
9. Allocates resources fairly and for their best use			
10. Uses clear criteria for job and performance evaluations			
11. Is considerate of the emotions of others			
12. Demonstrates the ability to manage his or her own emotions			
13. Exhibits respect for others			
14. Coaches and mentors others for their own development			
15. Is approachable and easy to talk to			
16. Listens to the opinions of others			
17. Actively seeks the opinions of others			
18. Communicates in an effective manner			
19. Gives honest and constructive feedback			

Comparison Sheet—continued

Characteristic	Average of peers and employees	Supervisor	Self
20. Thinks ahead and develops clear plans			
21. Makes sound decisions when under pressure			
22. Attempts to thoroughly assess a problem before taking action			
23. Is creative in solving problems			
24. Exhibits knowledge of his or her particular field			
25. Shares that knowledge with others			
26. Keeps informed of new material and changes in the field			
27. Is organized			
28. Has a good work ethic			
29. Demonstrates responsibility on the job			
30. Maintains a high energy level			
31. Admits to mistakes			
32. Accepts criticism			

List below any comments received in the evaluations that need consideration and attention.

_____

_____

_____

_____

_____

_____

_____

_____

_____

_____

_____

_____

_____

References

Anderson, A., L. Cohn, and T. Holbrook. *Making Weight.* California: Gurze Books, 2000.

Argyris, C. "Interpersonal Barriers to Decision Making." *Harvard Business Review on Decision Making.* Massachusetts: Harvard Business School Press, 1966, pp. 59–95.

Bargh, J. A., and T. L. Chartrand. "The Unbearable Automaticity of Being." *American Psychologist.* 1999, 54:462–479.

Bompa, T. O. *Periodization: Theory and Methodology of Training.* Illinois: Human Kinetics, 1999.

Bonanno, G. A. "Emotion Self-Regulation." In T. J. Mayne and G. A. Bonanno (Eds.), *Emotions: Current Issues and Future Directions.* New York: Guilford, 2001, pp. 251–285.

Buss, D. M. "The Evolution of Happiness." *American Psychologist.* 2000, 55:15–23.

Campbell, A. *The Sense of Well-Being in America.* New York: McGraw-Hill, 1981.

Collins, J. "Level 5 Leadership: The Triumph of Humility and Fierce Resolve." *Harvard Business Review.* 2001, 79:67–76.

Conger, J. A. "The Necessary Art of Persuasion." *Harvard Business Review on Managing People.* Massachusetts: Harvard Business School Press, 1998, pp. 227–255.

Conway, M., and M. Ross. "Getting What You Want by Revising What You Had." *Journal of Personality and Social Psychology.* 1984, 47:738–748.

Coren, S. *Sleep Thieves.* New York: Free Press, 1996.

Csikszentmihalyi, M. "If We Are So Rich, Why Aren't We Happy?" *American Psychologist.* 1999, 54:821–827.

Dement, W. C., and C. Vaughan. *The Promise of Sleep.* New York: Delacorte Press, 1999.

Diener, E. "Subjective Well-Being." *American Psychologist.* 2000, 55:34–43.

Foreyt, J. P., W. S. Poston, and G. K. Goodrick. "Future Directions in Obesity and Eating Disorders." *Addictive Behaviors.* 1996, 21:767–778.

Fredrickson, B. L. "What Good Are Positive Emotions?" *Review of General Psychology.* 1998, 2:300–319.

Fredrickson, B. L, and C. Branigan. "Positive Emotions." In T. J. Mayne and G. A. Bonanno (Eds.), *Emotions: Current Issues and Future Directions.* New York: Guilford, 2001, pp. 123–151.

Gagnon, S. "The Truth about Muscular Development." *Personal Fitness Professional.* 2001, 3:40–43.

Gallup, G. G., and F. Newport. "Americans Widely Disagree on What Constitutes Rich." *Gallup Poll Monthly.* July 1990, pp. 28–36.

Glassner, B. *The Culture of Fear: Why Americans Are Afraid of the Wrong Things.* New York: Basic Books, 1999.

Goleman, D. *Working with Emotional Intelligence.* New York: Bantam, 1998.

———*Emotional Intelligence.* New York: Bantam, 1995.

Goleman, D., R. Boyatzis, and A. McKee. *Primal Leadership.* Massachusetts: Harvard Business School Press, 2002.

Gortmaker, S. L., A. Must, J. M. Perrin, A. M. Sobol, and W. H. Dietz. "Social and Economic Consequences of Overweight in Adolescence and Young Adulthood." *New England Journal of Medicine.* 1993, 329:1008–1012.

Griffeth, R. W., and P. W. Hom. *Retaining Valued Employees.* California: Sage Publications, 2001.

Gross, J. J. "The Emerging Field of Emotion Regulation: An Integrative Review." *Review of General Psychology.* 1998, 2:271–299.

Hamer, D., and P. Copeland. *Living with Our Genes.* New York: Doubleday, 1998.

Hastie, R., and R. M. Dawes. *Rational Choice in an Uncertain World.* California: Sage Publications, 2001.

Hatfield, F. C. *Fitness: The Complete Guide.* California: International Sports Sciences Association, 1996.

Hawley, J., and L. Burke. *Peak Performance.* Australia: Allen and Unwin, 1998.

Hays, K. F. *Working It Out: Using Exercise in Psychotherapy.* Washington: American Psychological Association, 1999.

Hill, J. O., and J. C. Peters. "Environmental Contributions to the Obesity Epidemic." *Science.* 1998, 280:1371–1373.

Hoffman, D. D. *Visual Intelligence.* New York: Norton, 1998.

Hollander, E. P., and L. R. Offermann. "Power and Leadership in Organizations: Relationships in Transition." *American Psychologist.* 1990, 45:179–189.

Ikemi, Y., and S. Nakagawa. "A Psychosomatic Study of Contagious Dermatitis." *Kyoshu Journal of Medical Science.* 1962, 13:335–350.

Jensen, E. *Brain-Based Learning.* California: Turning Point Publishing, 1996.

Katz, J. H., and F. A. Miller. "Coaching Leaders through Culture Change." *Consulting Psychology Journal.* 1996, 48:104–114.

Keltner, D., and J. Haidt. "Social Functions of Emotions." In T. J. Mayne and G. A. Bonanno (Eds.), *Emotions: Current Issues and Future Directions.* New York: Guilford, 1996, pp. 192–213.

Keltner, D., and A. M. Kring. "Emotion, Social Function, and Psychopathology." *Review of General Psychology.* 1998, 2:320–342.

Kennedy-Moore, E., and J. C. Watson. *Expressing Emotion.* New York: Guilford, 1999.

Kiel, F., E. Rimmer, K. Willams, and M. Doyle. "Coaching at the Top." *Consulting Psychology Journal.* 1996, 48:67–77.

Kilburg, R. R. *Executive Coaching.* Washington: American Psychological Association, 2000.

Kotter, J. P. "What Leaders Really Do." In *Harvard Business Review on Leadership.* Massachusetts: Harvard Business School Press, 1990, pp. 37–60.

Langer, E. J. "The Illusion of Control." *Journal of Personality and Social Psychology.* 1975, 32:311–328.

Livingston, J. S. "Pygmalion in Management." In *Harvard Business Review on Managing People.* Massachusetts: Harvard Business School Press, 1988, pp. 45–72.

Loehr, J., and T. Schwartz. "The Making of a Corporate Athlete." *Harvard Business Review.* 2001, 79:120–128.

Luciano, L. *Looking Good: Male Body Image in Modern America.* New York: Hill and Wang, 2001.

Manzoni, J., and J. Barsoux. "The Set-Up-to-Fail Syndrome." In *Harvard Business Review on Managing People.* Massachusetts: Harvard Business School Press, 1998, pp. 197–226.

Mayne, T. J. "Emotions and Health." In T. J. Mayne and G. A. Bonanno (Eds.), *Emotions: Current Issues and Future Directions.* New York: Guilford, 2001, pp. 361–397.

Meehl, P. E. *Clinical versus Statistical Prediction: A Theoretical Analysis and a Review of the Evidence.* Minnesota: University of Minnesota Press, 1954.

Melcher, J., and G. J. Bostwick. "The Obese Client: Myths, Facts, Assessment, and Intervention." *Health and Social Work.* 1998, 23:195–202.

Mesquita, B. "Culture and Emotion: Different Approaches to the Question." In T. J. Mayne and G. A. Bonanno (Eds.), *Emotions: Current Issues and Future Directions.* New York: Guilford, 2001, pp. 214–250.

Mintzberg, H. "The Manager's Job: Folklore and Fact." In *Harvard Business Review on Leadership.* Massachusetts: Harvard Business School Press, 1975, pp. 1–36.

Morin, C. M. *Insomnia: Psychological Assessment and Management.* New York: Guilford, 1993.

Moskowitz, J. T. "Emotion and Coping." In T. J. Mayne and G. A. Bonanno (Eds.), *Emotions: Current Issues and Future Directions.* New York: Guilford, 2001, pp. 311–336.

Myers, D. G. "The Funds, Friends, and Faith of Happy People." *American Psychologist.* 2000, 55:56–67.

Nesse, R. M., and G. C. Williams. *Why We Get Sick.* New York: New York Times Books, 1994.

Nohria, N., and J. D. Berkley. "Whatever Happened to the Take-Charge Manager?" In *Harvard Business Review on Leadership.* Massachusetts: Harvard Business School Press, 1994, pp. 199–222.

Park, D. C. "Acts of Will?" *American Psychologist.* 1999, 54:461.

Peterson, C. "The Future of Optimism." *American Psychologist.* 2000, 55:44–55.

Pinker, S. *How the Mind Works.* New York: Norton, 1997.

"President's Council on Physical Fitness and Sports." *Fitness Fundamentals: Guidelines for Personal Exercise Programs.* On-line. Available: hoptechno.com/book11

Prochaska, J. O., and C. C. DiClemente. "Stages of Change in the Modification of Problem Behaviors." In M. Hersen, R. M. Eisler, and P. M. Miller (Eds.), *Progress in Behavior Modification.* Illinois: Sycamore Publishing Company, 1992, pp. 184–214.

———*The Transtheoretical Approach: Crossing Traditional Boundaries of Therapy.* Illinois: Dow Jones-Irwin, 1984.

Rechtschaffen, A. "The Control of Sleep." In W. A. Hunt (Ed.), *Human Behavior and its Control.* Massachusetts: Schenkman Publishing Company, 1971, pp. 75–92.

Roper Organization. [Untitled Survey]. *Public Opinion.* 1984, August/September, p. 25.

Rosenberg, E. L. "Levels of Analysis and the Organization of Affect." *Review of General Psychology.* 1998, 2:247–270.

Ryan, R. M., and E. L. Deci. "Self-Determination Theory and the Facilitation of Intrinsic Motivation, Social Development, and Well-Being." *American Psychologist.* 2000, 55:68–78.

Sawyer, J. "Measurement and Prediction, Clinical and Statistical." *Psychological Bulletin.* 1966, 66:178–200.

Sax, L. J., A. W. Astin, W. S. Korn, and K. M. Mahoney. *The American Freshman: National Norms for Fall 1998.* Los Angeles: Higher Education Research Institute, University of California, 1998.

Schwartz, B. "Self-Determination: The Tyranny of Freedom." *American Psychologist.* 2000, 55:79–88.

Seligman, M. E. *What You Can Change and What You Can't.* New York: Knopf, 1993.

Seligman, M. E., K. Reivich, L. Jaycox, and J. Gillham. *The Optimistic Child.* New York: Houghton Mifflin Company, 1995.

Seligman, M. E., and M. Csikszentmihalyi. "Positive Psychology: An Introduction." *American Psychologist.* 2000, 55:5–14.

Shelton, M. "The Perils of Promotion." *Camping Magazine.* 2001, 74:16–18.

———"The Psychology of Change." *Personal Fitness Professional.* 2000, 2:24–29.

Silver, R. L. *Coping with an Undesirable Life Event: A Study of Early Reactions to Physical Disability.* Unpublished doctoral dissertation, Evanston, Illinois: Northwestern University, 1982.

Smith, L. "The Executive's New Coach." *Fortune.* 1993, December 27:126–134.

Snyder, C. R. *The Psychology of Hope: You Can Get There from Here.* New York: Free Press, 1994.

Tjosvold, D. *Learning to Manage Conflict.* New York: Lexington Books, 1993.

Tversky, A., and D. Kahneman. "Judgments under Uncertainty: Heuristics and Biases." *Science.* 1974, 185:1124–1131.

———"Availability: A Heuristic for Judging Frequency and Probability." *Cognitive Psychology.* 1973, 5:207–232.

Valliant, G. E. *Adaptation to Life.* Massachusetts: Little and Brown, 1977.

Wedding, D., and D. Faust. "Clinical Judgment and Decision Making in Neuropsychology." *Archives of Clinical Neuropsychology.* 1989, 4:233–265.

Weisinger, H. *Emotional Intelligence at Work.* California: Jossey-Bass Publishers, 1998.

Wessler, R. L. "Cognitive Appraisal Therapy and Disorders of Personality." In K. T. Kuehlwein and H. Rosen (Eds.), *Cognitive Therapies in Action.* California: Jossey-Bass, 1993, pp. 240–267.

Wickelgren, I. "Obesity: How Big a Problem?" *Science.* 1998, 280:1364–1367.

Zaleznik, A. "Managers and Leaders: Are They Different?" In *Harvard Business Review on Leadership.* Massachusetts: Harvard Business School Press, 1977, pp. 61–88.

personal change and, 125–127
  camp director, 127–133
  retreat director, 127–133
  personal weaknesses, 134
  process overview, 128–130
  reviewing results, 132–133
  sample sheet, 177–180
  sample evaluation, 173–176
  self-evaluation, 132
evolutionary psychology, emotions and, 48
exaggeration of positive or negative, distorted thinking patterns and, 89–90
  mental capacity training, 163
exercise. See physical activity; physical exercise
expectations, managers and, 73
experience, 9
  components of, 9
  emotions and, 10, 11
  impulse control and, 10
  impulses and, 10
  introspection, 11
  physical reactions and, 10
  self-awareness and, 11
  sensations and, 10
  thoughts and, 10, 11
expertise, credibility and, 141
expressing emotions, 61–67
  anger, 65
    steps for, 65–66
  emotional capacity training session, 153, 155
  objectives, 64
extrinsic motivation, 118–119
  integrative capacity training session, 171

F

factual information level, communication, 69
  emotional capacity training session, 156
faith, psychological well-being and, 117
false memories, personal maps and, 94–95
fat intake, fitness lifestyle and, 21
fat loss, weight loss and, 20
fear, purpose, 54

feedback, 38
  emotional blind spot and, 52
  evaluations
    camp director, 128–130
    retreat director, 128–130
  evaluations and, 125–126
  supervisory sessions, 144
  training and, 143
feelings level, communication, 69
figurehead role, 3–4
fitness lifestyle, 16. See also weight; weight loss
  appearance and, 16
  athletic performance and, 16
  body composition analysis and, 20
  cosmetic change and, 17
  eating plan, 17
  effects of extra weight, 18
  general fitness and, 16
  goals and, 16
  healthy eating plan, 20–22
  insurance weight tables, 18
  meals, number of, 22
  media influences on choices, 17
  permanent weight loss, 19
  physical activity and, 23–28
  physical capacity training session, 147–148
  rest, 30–32
  stress management, 28
  weight-loss, products, 17
flexibility training, 25
flexibility with emotions, developing, 58–59
flow, psychological well-being and, 120–121
fluid loss, weight loss and, 20
follow-up to training, 143
followers, 7
  effect on leaders, 2
  presence of, 2
four internal experiences, 9

G

general fitness vs. athletic performance, 16
general leadership training session, 145–147

genetic design, weight and, 22

genetic links to weight, 18–19

genetics, muscle development and, 25

goals
fitness lifestyle and, 16
goal-directed information, attention and, 76
leaders and, 2
physical exercise, 27

H

happiness
biology and, 108
competitiveness and, 109
environmental conditions and, 111
loss and, 110
money and, 112–114
negative emotions and, 109
negative experiences and, 108
obstacles to, 108–114
positive experiences and, 108
satisfaction and, 108
social support and, 111
variety of emotion, 109

health
anger and, 54
fitness lifestyle, 16–32
physical activity, 23–27
physical capacity and, 13–15, 22–23
physical capacity training session, 147–148
self-esteem and, 14
sleep and, 30–32
stress, 28–30
weight, 18–20

health & fitness information, 15

healthy eating, 20–22

high-performance pyramid, physical capacity and, 13

hiring, based on feelings, 49

hope, psychological well-being and, 117

hostility, emotional set point and, 46

humanists, positive psychology and, 107

I

illness, physical capacity and, 14

impulse control, experience and, 10

impulses, experience and, 10

inborn qualities, 1, 7

inborn traits, emotions and, 39

individual supervision. *See* supervisory sessions

information, importance, attention and, 76

inspiration, leaders and, 2

insurance weight tables, 18

integrative capacity training session
motivation, 171–172
optimism, 168–171

integrative factors. *See also* spiritual capacity
know thyself (evaluations), 121–122
Level 5 leadership, 122–123
obstacles to happiness, 108–114
positive psychology, 106–107

interest, purpose, 55

internal experiences, positive psychology and, 107

interpretation
optimistic thinking and, 116
pessimistic thinking and, 116
speed and accuracy and, 79

intervention, personal change and, 135

interviews
cognitive limits and, 77
small environments, 3

intrinsic motivation, 118–119
integrative capacity training session, 171

introspection, experience and, 11

itching eyes, sleep deprivation and, 31

J–K

jealousy, purpose, 54

job satisfaction, 6
supervisors and, 37

know thyself (evaluations), integrative factors, 121–122

positive stress, 28–29

Post-Traumatic Stress Disorder, 29

power, anger and, 57

precontemplation, personal change and, 136

preparation, personal change and, 137–138

presence of followers, 2

privileged information, leader and, 4

problem solving, 100–101
  positive stress and, 29

problem-focused response to stress, 29

process of personal change, 133–142
  action, 138–139
  contemplation, 137
  maintenance, 140
  precontemplation, 136
  preparation, 137–138

productivity, rest and, 32

professional athletes, physical exercise and, 24

progression, exercise program and, 26

psychological well-being, 114
  faith and, 117
  flow and, 120–121
  hope and, 117
  motivation and, 118–119
  optimism and, 115
  physical activity, 23
  relationships and, 117

psychology, 105
  cognitive, 107
  evolutionary psychology, 48
  positive psychology, 106–107

psychology of emotions, 39–41

purposes of emotions, 48
  anger, 55
  disgust, 54
  emotional capacity training session, 152
  fear, 54
  interest, 55
  jealousy, 54
  love, 55
  lust, 54
  satisfaction, 55

R

randomness
  cognitive therapy and, 97–98
  decision making and, 85–86

ranges of emotion, 42

rational choice, decision making and, 98–100

reaction time, sleep deprivation and, 31

reasoning ability, sleep deprivation and, 32

recognition, automatic thoughts and (distorted thinking patterns), 163–164

recognizing emotions, training session, 149–151

regulating emotion, 59–61
  present emotions, 61

relationships
  coaching and, 144
  credibility and, 141
  psychological well-being and, 117
  training and, 144

resource allocator role, leaders, 4–6

resources, availability, situational leadership and, 2

respect, emotions and, 37

response modulation, regulating emotions and, 60–61

rest
  physical activity and, 32
  physical capacity training session, 149
  productivity and, 32
  sleep, 30–31

retreat director, evaluations, 127–133

risk takers, emotional set point and, 46

roles
  conflict, 1
  disseminator, 4
  disturbance handler, 4
  entrepreneur, 4
  examples, 5–6
  figurehead, 3–4
  general leadership training session, 146
  integration, 1
  leaders, 3
  leaders vs. managers, 2